OF NO REPUTATION - AN ORDINARY LIFE

Of No Reputation
An Ordinary Life

Stephen Grant

JOHN RITCHIE LTD
CHRISTIAN PUBLICATIONS

40 Beansburn, Kilmarnock, Scotland

ISBN-13: 978 1 909803 92 3

www.ritchiechristianmedia.co.uk

All scripture references are from the New King James Version.

Typeset by John Ritchie Ltd., Kilmarnock
Printed by Bell & Bain Ltd., Glasgow

Contents

Introduction

I know for many of you it is hard to imagine but I can remember a life before Facebook. I actually lived without wireless broadband, touch screens and I am old enough to have endured the frustration of dial up modems. Is it possible that I grew up in a home with one TV that had the grand total of 3 channels? My teenage years were all about having a Commodore 64 or a Sinclair Spectrum when Alan Sugar was famous for Amstrad and not The Apprentice. I am so old I listened to music on vinyl and thought that a Walkman was beyond cool.

It now seems incredible that I was alive when mobile phones were non-existent and people wrote letters with a pen. My children can't believe that I wrote to their mother and had to wait for a few days for her response to drop into my mailbox at West Park Halls of Residence in Dundee. It may seem old fashioned but there is something wonderfully personal about unfolding the page and seeing the familiar handwriting in a letter.

In some ways this year is a turning point. I was 22 years old when Sharon and I married and we have recently celebrated our 22nd wedding anniversary. To my children I am old and to my parents I seem to be catching them. I am slowly coming to terms with the creaky knees and slower reactions of a middle aged 5-a-side football player.

I became a Christian when I was a young boy. I knelt at the side of my bed with my older brother as my mother led us to the Lord in prayer. In my memory it was a Tuesday night after the "Happy Hour", which now seems the strangest name to give a children's Bible Club. The feeling of relief and joy as I stared up at the top bunk bed is a vivid memory (I always had the lower bunk as the youngest brother, just one of the inevitable consequences of sibling birth order).

I don't think I had great ambitions at that early age and if I did it is unlikely that they would have extended beyond the world of Bridge of Weir Primary School or winning the Saturday afternoon long game of football with my friends down at "the Glen". Life was simple, happy and carefree.

I was baptised at 14, having waited for a year. David Stevely, my best friend and colleague in many a scrape, had come back from the same Christian Youth Camp wanting to be baptised. I didn't want to be seen to copy him, so I waited. I suppose it was the first serious decision I made as a Christian. I remember that it was a big deal to me. I took the bread and wine at the Lord's supper for the first time the following Sunday and felt part of something bigger than the group of 40 or so Christians meeting in Hope Hall, Bridge of Weir.

It all seems very distant now. I read books of the Bible in one sitting, propped up at the end of my bed, back against the radiator, eating bag after bag of crisps. I watched my dad as he came out of his study before going to his work and disappeared back in there after work. Long hours of Bible study and preaching were his "hobbies" and I thought that this was the man that I would be; I didn't doubt it for a moment. In the meantime, I decided to dedicate myself to having a good time as a boy before I became a man. Sport became my God and I was good at it. I played tennis, squash, football, basketball, volleyball and any other sport I could find in school and regional teams, revelling in the sheer joy of competition. I loved to play and win. I trained hard, spending hours at the tennis club on my own hitting against a practice wall. Red ash was the ground upon which I worshipped.

My student years took me to Dundee when I was 17 and I left 4 years later with a degree, a fiancé and ambition. I had been introduced to Christians in Dundee and Perth who were streets ahead of me in their Bible knowledge and Christian experience. I realised that I was ignorant of God and His Word and I wanted to change that. I still have the Strong's concordance Ian Mathers bought for me at the CLC bookshop in Aberdeen and the Vine's Dictionary purchased in Dundee. These were the first building blocks of Bible study. My Schofield bible was traded in for a Newberry and I thought that I was on my way. I studied my Bible harder than my degree course and spent many a long night cross checking words and agonising over smelly second hand books. I found real pleasure in hunting around second hand bookshops with my favourite being the Church of Scotland bookshop on Buchanan Street, Glasgow. It is hard to describe the joy of finding a good copy of Trench's Synonyms and not sound like a real nerd. These were the days before the internet and free Bible study resources. I wouldn't change a moment of that time. It was a new world opening up to me as I read the works of these great scholars, getting to grips with majestic Biblical truth. Hard earned truth stays in the sticky side of the brain and I still have clear recall of moments when the penny dropped and God taught me shape, structure and the flow of truth through scripture, all in the quietness of my room as I burned the midnight oil.

I was 18 when I began to preach and discovered that the nerves quickly receded. I was soon busy every weekend in various places preaching on a Sunday and through the week. I loved preaching and read the books that all young preachers read. I was going to be Jim Elliot, Spurgeon and a bit of Wesley thrown in for good measure. I read about the great missionaries and martyrs and marvelled that we shared the same task and preached from the same text. I was part of something big and I was ambitious.

I got married, got a job, became a dad and continued to preach. I was still ambitious. I had goals and they were big. When I was 29 I left my job and began preaching full time. I clearly remember driving north from Ayrshire on the A77 and coming over a hill to see Glasgow spread out before me. I can still feel the sense of mission and passion I felt for this city with its teeming multitudes. I remember the burden of working out how I could accomplish the evangelization of a city. Before long my plans formed and faded, time came and went and Glasgow remained as dark as ever: "Let Glasgow flourish through the preaching of his word and the praising of his name" the long forgotten city motto.

As I write this I am sitting in a Starbucks at Braehead, Glasgow, which is a relatively new shopping centre. I am

44 and growing old with the wife of my youth. We have 3 children who are racing through their teenage years. Over these last 30 years I have written, taught, mentored and preached. I have been a son, brother, husband, dad, uncle, evangelist, friend and church elder. I have grown in some areas of character and relationship with God and I am not the same as I was, but I am also not that much different, certainly not 30 years worth of difference. The inescapable and honest conclusion must be that my life has been very ordinary. I am not Spurgeon, Wesley or Jim Elliot and am unlikely to morph into them any time soon.

Compared to some of the life stories I read as a young man my life has been unremarkable and that sometimes troubles me as I begin to feel the shift of time. I am not a particularly contemplative person neither do I spend an inordinate amount of time gazing into the middle distance with moist eyes. I am quite content, most of the time, to be unremarkable and to have a life that is mundane and ordinary but some of the time I am not. There are moments when I wish for better, wish that I had done better; preached like Spurgeon, written like John Piper, even died like Jim Elliot. I feel I have fallen short by being unremarkable and ordinary. I haven't changed the world for Jesus. I haven't even changed my street for Jesus. I suppose I am one of the 99% of present day Christians who are more like the people who received Paul's epistles than like the Apostle who wrote them.

Over the years I have read many inspirational books which tend to focus on exceptional people who have done unusual things for God. We read about overcoming tragedy or coping with disability and marvel at the strength, resourcefulness and faith of people who endure. The evangelisation of a community and remarkable growth of a church pokes and prods at our conscience and usually makes us feel inadequate as we think of our church or witness for God. Then we get up on a Monday morning, join the rush hour traffic, have a strong coffee, punch our card, fill in our time sheet, work the day, make our way home, dinner, kids, doze, bed. There only seems to be time for inspirational living at the weekend.

There is a stage in life when we should dream. It is one of the glories of youth that life stretches as a blank canvas and you stand poised with brush in hand waiting for inspiration. During these years you form opinions that harden into convictions. People influence you in all sorts of ways and you go through wonderfully idealistic stages. You have time and no baggage. Your mind is free of regrets and you have no idea of your limitations. It is a great time of life. That is when you pick up causes and spend some of that seemingly endless energy doing your bit to end world poverty, protect the environment, care for goats in South America, go and work in a school or build a well in an African village. You could be on the streets of your city in the wee small hours at the weekend with a soup kitchen or volunteering in a hospice shop. This is the period of your life when you can do good work in a charitable sphere. It is the time before responsibility crowds in and squeezes time and energy. It is better to get involved in such good works when you are young rather than waste your early years in front of a screen or sleeping.

I have travelled to Indonesia for six years visiting a group of Christians in a small church. When I first met them they had only been saved for a relatively short time. They had gone to work illegally in a Korean factory and heard the Gospel from a Korean evangelist. Five friends were saved, baptized and became part of a local church. They were able to stay in Korea and work due to an amnesty for illegal workers. After a couple of years they came back to Indonesia and set up businesses in a suburb of Jakarta, starting a small New Testament Church. It was in these early years that I first met them and travelled to the house in which they met as a church. It was like a student flat. The five young men stayed in the house, got up early and ran, studied their Bibles and prayed before going to work in their shops. When the day was over they came back to the house and ate together, finishing the day with more prayer. They had energy, zeal and spiritual ambition to do great things for God. In the house there was a table tennis table, weights and clothes everywhere.

Six years on and fourteen visits later it is a different picture. There are more people in the Church. Some of them are now married with families and as a result they don't all live together or go for a run in the morning. Family life and church responsibilities have brought their own routines as they shepherd the flock that God has given them. They are now living ordinary, quiet lives. There is no less zeal or ambition to bring the Gospel to their community but there is a growing maturity that is appropriate to their spiritual experience. Having watched the progress of my brothers and sisters in the Jakarta area I can see the inevitable shift that responsibility brings. Having to earn money to feed your family and help others brings its own baggage. Your mind becomes cluttered, anxieties distract and cause you to fret. Priorities shift and life solidifies from the fluidity of youth to the harder path of maturity. It is inevitable and it is right.

I have ridden through Borneo jungles with these young men, teeth rattling and head bouncing off the roof of a jeep, during endless miles of red dirt. I have played football with them in the sweltering heat and eaten lots of street food. We have debated, discussed and worshipped together as we travelled many miles in a minivan experiencing our own "Boys Own" adventure. For them these days are passing as they have children, responsibility, family routine and church responsibilities. Does this mean that their days of doing great things for God are over? Not so, they might just be commencing. It is no less satisfying to God to see them working hard and raising their families as travelling into Borneo with the Gospel, it is just different. We will see that one is as powerful a testimony as the other and God is able to use both to accomplish His purpose.

Please do not think that I am suggesting that it is wrong to be inspired by outstanding people. I am not advocating a lack of respect or interest in men and women who have been used by God to do exceptional things. Hebrews ch11 draws our attention to the historical roll call of faith in order for us to find strength to go on for God. You could hardly read that chapter without admiring these men and women and the great things God accomplished in their lives. However, don't forget that Paul also had his own roll call at the end of many of his letters. You read the names of men and women who are mentioned in scripture but have no exceptional qualities or achievements linked to their names. It seems that many of them were ordinary people who lived ordinary lives for God. They ran businesses, raised families, stayed in the same area and poured a lifetime of energy and commitment into the same local church. They were soldiers who lived for God in the army, mothers who raised children for God, tax collectors, tent makers, businessmen and women, civil servants, slaves, fishermen, and farmers grafting and toiling to make ends meet and provide for their families. They were raising children and looking after parents, getting by and keeping their heads above water. In those circumstances of normal life they were living for God and that is what He wanted them to do. They were shining lights in streets of spiritual darkness. They were upright, hard working, kind, clean living, joyful, quiet and effective testimonies to God. They didn't become famous or recognised beyond their immediate work and social environment. They were the people Warren Wiersbe wrote about in his book "In Praise Of Plodders".

This book is not about setting you on fire for God or stirring you to great and noble deeds. It is not my intention to produce missionaries, media personalities, poets, preachers or standout people. I want to stir another ambition, something that is not usually associated with aspirational writing but is expressed by Paul as he wrote to the Thessalonian Christians: "But concerning brotherly love you have no need that I should write to you, for you yourselves are taught by God to love one another; and indeed you do so toward all the brethren who are in all Macedonia. But we urge you, brethren, that you increase more and more; that you also aspire to lead a quiet life, to mind your own business, and to work with your own hands, as we commanded you, that you may walk properly toward those who are outside, and that you may lack nothing (1 Thessalonians 4:9-12).

CHAPTER ONE

Ordinary or Mundane

I have listened to a lot of sermons but I have only once heard someone begin with the unforgettable and incongruous words "Humpty Dumpty sat on a wall ...". This was why my son Andrew asked Jeremy Singer to speak at his baptism. It is hardly surprising that Jeremy held the attention of everyone present, both young and old.

Jeremy reminded us of Humpty Dumpty's conversation with Alice in "Through the Looking Glass" written by Lewis Carroll. "When I use a word," Humpty Dumpty said, in rather a scornful tone, "it means just what I choose it to mean -- neither more nor less." "The question is," said Alice, "whether you can make words mean so many different things." "The question is" said Humpty Dumpty, "which is to be master -- that's all."

Humpty Dumpty is saying that he can stipulate the definition of a term. Lewis Carroll was a Professor of Logic and Mathematics and elaborated on the theme in his work "Symbolic Logic", "I maintain that any writer of a book is fully authorized in attaching any meaning he likes to any word he intends to use. If I find an author saying at the beginning of his book, 'Let it be understood that by the word white I shall always mean black' I meekly accept his ruling, however injudicious I may think it." Jeremy helpfully pointed out to us that when it comes to the Bible, God is the author and it is His meaning that is relevant.

In light of Lewis Carroll's plea for consistency of word usage and meaning, I thought about a couple of words which I have used and realised I should check whether I was being like Humpty Dumpty.

So here is the question: Is "ordinary" the same as "mundane"?

Before I looked at a dictionary I just shut my eyes and tried to get opposite words. I came up with "exceptional" for ordinary and "exciting" for mundane. I thought about colours that might represent the words and came up with "beige" for ordinary and "beige" for mundane. The process wasn't working well so I resorted to Google. That was more productive and gave me what I already suspected; there is a subtle difference in the words that is important for our purpose.

Ordinary is "commonplace or standard". My thanks to Google for that precise definition. Lewis Carroll would approve because I am going to adopt that definition for our purpose. When I refer to an ordinary life it is the commonplace or standard Christian life that God teaches us about in the Bible. Google have helpfully provided some synonyms that expand the definition, "usual, normal, habitual, customary". For the avoidance of doubt, these are good words that may, at first glance, seem a bit boring and uninspiring but we shall see otherwise.

Mundane is "(a) lacking interest and excitement; dull (b) of this earthly world rather than a heavenly or spiritual one". I am not going to pretend that this was the definition that I expected. It actually took me a little by surprise to read the words "earthly, heavenly and spiritual" in a Google definition. The synonyms increased my interest, "worldly, temporal, secular, terrestrial".

There is a clear difference between a life that is mundane and one that is ordinary. For a Christian an ordinary life does not lack excitement or interest and should not be dull. We shall see that the Bible teaches us that there is a spiritual dimension to every aspect of our lives which is not restricted to earth or constrained by time. My life may be ordinary but that does not mean that it is mundane. In fact, on the basis of our definitions, as a Christian my life cannot be mundane as so much of it is not of this world. Jesus Christ my Lord and Saviour is in Heaven along with my hope, my inheritance, my Father and all of my spiritual blessings. I know that I am part of a great story that is being worked out in a spiritual realm in accordance with the will of God. I may at times lose perspective and think that the things I see and hear are all important, I may even forget about God, never pray to my Father and forget about the spiritual enemies which the Bible describes, but that is only my lack of focus and perception. It does not alter the truth that my citizenship is in heaven (Phil 3:20) and God has blessed me with every spiritual blessing in the heavenly places in Christ (Eph1:3).

It is the joy of youth to dream and imagine what could be. But really, only a few of us have the ability to be nuclear scientists or even to get the grades that will open up career

21

opportunities into high powered, high earning careers. Most of us settle for low to middle income jobs. We move to an area and quickly settle down into routine. We get married and have families. We take on responsibility that anchors us to employment and the care of people who depend upon us. We quickly start to live ordinary lives.

Our service for the Lord is much the same. When we are young Christians we dream of being missionaries and high achievers; following the Lord wherever He will lead us, not for one minute expecting that He would lead us to that factory down the road, the taxi, shop or office. We may have seen ourselves as blazing lights in a dark place making our mark for God, not really anticipating that the biggest work for God in which we will ever be involved will take place in our own hearts.

Some of us are good at being ordinary and some are not. There are people who struggle with routine and seem to need change. They tend to move around a lot, changing jobs always looking for a better opportunity and a quick fix to financial pressure. There are people who are like "fiddlers elbows"; they go up and down all the times, experiencing times of great success and other times of low depression. They can just as easily blaze like a shooting star or crash and burn. It is the difference between being mercurial and ordinary.

God has used people who were changeable. Elijah stood on a mountain and faced down hundreds of pagan prophets, a very fierce King and an even scarier Queen. He shone brightly for God. He was outstanding, a hero, magnificent, inspirational in his courage and accomplishments. He was also depressed and self absorbed when he came off the mountaintop. He ran and hid from the very people whom he had withstood so publicly.

Peter was also a man of great courage. When he stated his determination to die for the Lord Jesus I have no doubt he meant it with all his heart. In fact, he got his sword out and started brandishing it in front of a hostile group of soldiers in Gethsemane. He was a leader who even walked on water towards the Lord Jesus in the middle of a storm. This was an outstanding man. Yet, this was the man who denied the Lord with oaths and curses when a young girl asked him some questions. This was the man whom Paul withstood to the face because his convictions had buckled before the men from Jerusalem and he wouldn't eat with Christians from a non-Jewish background.

There is no doubt that God used Elijah and Peter to do mighty things. However, it would be a mistake to think that God wants us all to be like Peter and Elijah. Elijah had to learn that while he was being used by God to do extraordinary things, there were 7,000 men in Israel who had not bowed the knee to Baal and were living quietly for God. For every Peter and Paul there were numerous disciples and later congregations of Christians who did not go on missionary journeys and turn the world upside down.

Ordinary is good as far as God is concerned. An ordinary life for God will never be mundane; it cannot be mundane. It is a life that is intimately connected to Heaven with spiritual components and character. An ordinary life is beautiful to God. I have known people who are up and down like the Grand old Duke of York's men, "And when they were up, they were up, And when they were down, they were down". Stability is important and along with that goes routine, which is essential. In order to please God we need to do small things regularly and not big things occasionally. We will see from the Bible that a testimony for God in our community, work place or family does not happen overnight but is built by consistent integrity in the ordinary things of life. A shooting star may be spectacular but only for a brief moment and then it is gone. It is better to be a city set on a hill or a lamp on a lampstand (Matt 5:14-15).

CHAPTER TWO

Satan Disturbs Our Ordinary Lives

Satan is a subtle enemy. Although his methods have not changed since the beginning of time, he has had thousands of years to perfect his work. When he began assaulting mankind in the Garden of Eden he was introduced as being "more cunning than any beast of the field which the LORD God had made" (Genesis 3:1). His sophisticated temptations and opposition to God in the 21st Century are only shiny versions of his original "modus operandi" displayed in Genesis Chapter 3.

By the time Satan turns up to speak to Eve, God has created a wonderful life for Adam and Eve and is enjoying a close relationship with them. "Then God blessed them, and God said to them, "Be fruitful and multiply; fill the earth and subdue it; have dominion over the fish of the sea, over the birds of the air, and over every living thing that moves on the earth" (Genesis 1:28).

Adam and Eve settled into an ordinary life. It could hardly be described as mundane since they received regular visits from the Lord who came down and walked with them in the cool of the day. They were living in the same place, serving the Lord, exercising their dominion over creation and enjoying their relationship with the Lord. It was perfect. Since sin had not entered into their hearts and minds they didn't get bored or discontented. Envy, jealousy, ambition were all foreign to them in their ordinary lives. Ordinary was good. Ordinary satisfied them and pleased God.

When Satan turned up everything changed. It is interesting that Satan's temptations created within Eve discontent with God's provision. Suddenly it was not enough. God was not enough. She wanted to have what belonged to God and to become like God. Her perspective changed and ordinary was not good enough anymore. To Eve, ordinary had become second rate.

Very few of us will ever experience a direct assault from Satan in the same way that Eve did in the Garden. However, we are involved in a conflict with spiritual wickednesses which bear the character of their master and use his methods. He is the Prince of the power of the air and has created a world culture which is anti God and actively opposes us as the children of God. The world's opposition to Christians is often a variation of the direct and blatant Satanic approach in the Garden of Eden.

Let's examine the conversation that took place between Satan and Eve.

Now the serpent was more cunning than any beast of the field which the LORD God had made. And he said to the woman, "Has God indeed said, 'You shall not eat of every tree of the garden'?"
(Genesis 3:1)

Satan asks the first question in the Bible. He is careful with his language when he speaks about God. After the description of the original creation in Genesis 2:4 God is referred to as "Lord God". If you are reading this book with a Bible handy then have a look at the following references and the consistent use of "Lord God" (chs 2:4, 5, 7, 8, 9, 18, 19, 21, 22, 3:1, 8, 9, 13, 14, 21, 22, 23...). The title emphasises the absolute authority of God and is a reminder to Satan of the central cause of his long warfare against God and men created in the image and likeness of God. Satan never calls God, "Lord God". This is a raw nerve and you get the impression that he would choke on the words rather than utter them.

Satan asked Eve a sophisticated question that would not be out of place in a 21st Century YouTube debate about God. We seem to think that we are intellectually sophisticated and advanced in education, philosophy and science. We feel we approach subjects such as Faith, Salvation, God, Eternity etc. in a more modern way than previous generations and arrive at conclusions which are mature and informed. We actually flatter ourselves and do a disservice to the generations that have gone before. As the Bible states, there is nothing new under the sun. We only have different technologies to express and explore what has always been.

Satan quotes the Lord God to Eve but as you would expect he manipulates the words in order to tempt her. God had actually said, "Of every tree of the garden you may freely eat; but of the tree of the knowledge of good and evil you shall not eat, for in the day that you eat of it you shall surely die" (Genesis 2:16, 17). Now where is the difference? Compare the two statements for a moment and consider what Satan is doing. God had said that every tree in the garden was available apart from the tree of the knowledge of good and evil. Adam and Eve are being directed to consider the vast provision that God had made for them and their freedom of enjoyment. The prohibition is tiny in light of the provision and is actually part of the blessing for them, protecting them from the terrible consequences of death.

Satan inverts the emphasis by saying, "look at all these trees but God will not let you eat of them all". He emphasizes "not eating" and by so doing causes Eve to think that God is not a bountiful God, He is a mean God of restriction. He has created this garden but he will not let Adam and Eve enjoy it all. He is keeping something from them. The implication is that God is preventing you from enjoying some great delight and restricting your freedom. If you could only break free from God's restriction then you would have total freedom and full enjoyment.

Satan is tempting Eve to a point of restless dissatisfaction with her ordinary life. He implies that in order to find true fulfilment she needs to do something radical, out of the ordinary and step over the boundaries that God had set in place. For the few among us whom God has gifted and raised up to do what seems to us as extraordinary things, that is their ordinary life. That is the boundary that God has set them; it is the sphere of their labour for God, it is the ordinariness of their life. The point is not so much what we do for God but whether we are content with the circumstances in which God has placed us and the service he has given us to fulfil. For Spurgeon it was preaching to tens of thousands, for Jim Elliot it ended with his death on a beach in Equador. For many of us it is raising a family, holding down a job, serving in our local assembly and witnessing in our community. The problem arises when we think there is more for us than God has given. When that thought arises and takes a hold in our minds, we are in trouble.

This is the battleground of the ages. You either believe Satan or God. Who is telling the truth? Who provides complete satisfaction and joy? This is one of the big obstacles that Satan has constructed to the Gospel. A life of sin is portrayed in the media and throughout society as being attractive, with no limits. You are your own God and you can do whatever you want as long as you don't bother other people. There is no such thing as absolute right or wrong and you can't be judged by anyone. This is freedom. This is a life that is never ordinary, dull, beige.

If we can't have this life ourselves then we can enjoy it vicariously through the media in the lives of celebrities. We can feast upon their sin and dramatic, mercurial existences as they soar into the stratosphere of fame and crash and burn along the way. Sin is rewarded with fast cars, big boats and exciting lifestyles. The temptation is set before us everyday with the fame and fortune of celebrities dominating news cycles and filling the airwaves. This is what is possible, this is what we should aim for, this should be your ambition.

On the other hand a life with God is portrayed as restrictive, boring and dull. To be content with God is tantamount to an admission of intellectual weakness. How could any thinking, educated and 21st Century person possibly be truly content with God alone?

Tragically, Satan deceived Eve. You can see the change in her thinking expressed in her response to Satan. "We may eat the fruit of the trees of the garden" (Genesis 3:2). She drops the "all" from what the Lord God had said and by so doing is slowly diminishing the extent of God's provision. She then adds something, "but of the fruit of the tree which is in the midst of the garden, God has said, 'You shall not eat it, nor shall you touch it, lest you die'"(Genesis 3:3). God had not mentioned touching the tree. Satan's subtle approach has paid off and in her mind she has fallen for it. She is thinking less of what God has provided and building up the restriction that God placed upon them into something more than it was.

The outcome of Satan's success in Eden was the entrance of sin into the world with all the dreadful consequences that followed. Adam and Eve lost their ordinary lives with God and never recovered them. The intimacy they had enjoyed with the Lord was lost as they were banished from His presence and required a covering for their sin and shame. Their family was destroyed when Cain murdered Abel. Death arrived sooner than they anticipated. Satan was proved to be the liar and you can imagine how much they longed for that ordinary life which was now an increasingly distant memory.

As you read through the historical sections of the Bible this seems to be a recurring theme. The people of God get fed up with their ordinary life with God and are dazzled by the thought of the unattainable: Israel rejecting the manna as they yearned after the food of Egypt (Numbers ch11), building a golden calf at the foot of Sinai (Exodus ch32), and calling for a King to be like all the nations round about them (1 Samuel ch8). The gods, kings and food of their enemies distracted them. It seems a bit bizarre that they should be so desperate to reject God and his leadership, not to mention free daily food raining down from heaven. God gave them social structure that included a sacrificial system enabling them to have a relationship with Him and experience His presence among them. They had the opportunity of living simple, routine lives that would have been the source of tremendous joy and blessing for them as a nation. God was providing for them in every way and their obedience was the key for full and unfettered joy. During the few seasons under good kings they experienced the fruit of such obedience. The regular three times a year national festivals at Jerusalem attracted the people as they came to worship God. The law of God was revered and they enjoyed peace and prosperity. But it never lasted. You soon read of a King who hankered after the gods of the nations around them or who broke down the national routine of worship and led the people into sin.

As I thought about that cycle of temptation, sin, repentance and recovery that recurs so often in the Old Testament, I wondered if that basic tendency to discontentment lies at the root of my recurring failure as a Christian. I can readily identify with the perplexing cycle of sin. I experience the frustration and self-pity that failure often brings. I have sat quietly with a deep sense of irritation at myself for not being satisfied with God or the ordinary life which I know is the basis of my most happy periods of life. John Piper was right to bring Jonathan Edward's ministry to our generation and speak of Christian Hedonism, "God is most glorified in me when I am most satisfied with Him". I know that is true but knowing it and living it are two different things. I go along for a while and then I get dazzled, or perhaps distracted even bored, if truth be told, and have to start all over again. When that happens Satan has won again, just as he did with Eve. He has caused me to diminish the goodness of God and exaggerate the restrictions of scripture to a point where I resist them. My perspective is distorted and that is when I am vulnerable.

Throughout history Satan has tried to disturb the ordinary lives of God's people by the extremes of violent persecution, intellectual philosophy, scientific education, not forgetting the insertion of false teachers into churches. However, it seems that his most effective approach has always been the carrot rather than the stick. This is essentially the story of Eden. The fruit of the tree of the knowledge of good and evil was hardly likely to be a carrot but the idea is the same. It worked with Demas when he left the Apostle Paul because he loved this present age. For most of us this is our spiritual battlefield. We won't be blazing trails through jungles with the Gospel. I don't think many of us will be standing before stadiums to preach or have ministries bearing our name or tag line. We will be fighting our spiritual battle in the quietness of our own circumstances trying to maintain a settled contentment with God and His will for our lives and doing so as we go to work, do the housework, take the kids to school, clean up the garden and balance the household budget. I think that in our prosperous, ambitious, materialistic, sophisticated, get rich and famous world we are effectively tempted by Satan to the point of dissatisfaction with our ordinary Christian lives.

CHAPTER THREE

Spiritual Disciplines

I have always admired writers and preachers who come up with a snappy title for their work. Sometimes I stumble upon a pithy heading and have to smother a small feeling of smugness when it sees the light of day. It seems that if you can have a short, interesting or even witty title you are well on your way to engaging a reader. I don't think that was always true of Christian writers. When you read some of the sermon titles from hundreds of years ago they seem to be long and complicated.

I came across a tongue twister title for a book when I was researching some of the Puritan writers. How about this for brevity and wit, "The Middle Things, In Reference to the First and Last Things: or, The Means, Duties, Ordinances, both Secret, Private and Public, for Continuance and Increase of a Godly Life, (Once Begun,) Till We Come to Heaven"? Isaac Ambrose was the writer. I don't think a publisher would have been thrilled with it today. However it was 1650 and he managed to have it reprinted twice over the following 7 years. Ambrose was writing about a subject that was important to the Puritan Christians of that age. They placed great emphasis upon spiritual disciplines as the foundation of their walk with the Lord. We could learn a lot from their writings on this subject. In truth, the foundation of a contented Christian life is built with some of the blocks of spiritual disciplines that were so precious to the Puritans. These are the things that are sometimes highlighted in the lives of famous men and women of God as the secret of their faith and endurance. What was true of them is true for all of us.

I left my job as a solicitor when I was 29 and since then have worked from home or in other people's homes. My new vocation required me to impose structure on my working day. I have no daily commute other than the walk to my study from my bedroom. I don't have to battle traffic and end up all stressed and bothered due to the lack of parking spaces before my week begins. I manage my own diary and arrange my schedule without reference to a supervisor or manager. There are often unexpected changes to my plans but I usually organise my own time. When I was thinking about spiritual disciplines in my life it is quite different for me now than it was when I worked in Glasgow. It was somehow harder when your day began with a trudge to the office in the pouring rain through a dark February morning.

One of the big issues that I remember having to face was the apparent disconnect between my spiritual weekend world and the one I entered on Monday morning. Reading my Bible and praying on Sunday morning fitted well into that day. My mind was focused on the Lord's Supper or the preaching that I would be involved in later that day. Saturdays were much the same as we often went to a Bible teaching conference or to socialise with Christians. At the weekend my head would be clearer and I would be less anxious to get going and get out the house to get stuff done. During the week my head was clouded with cases I was conducting and courts I had to visit. I was more concerned about speaking to Sheriff Crone of Kilmarnock Sheriff Court or Sheriff Mitchell at Glasgow Sheriff Court than meditating on Hebrews Chapter 3.

I prayed in the car on my way to work and sometimes wondered what other people thought as they saw me seemingly talking to myself in the long traffic jams on the M8 motorway. I regularly knew that feeling of guilt and failure as the week wore on with my Bible unopened and my head seldom bowed in prayer. The ideal beginning of a day often passed me by in the frantic morning rush and as for the tranquil prayer and Bible reading in the evening, that was mostly a weary flop into bed, token verse read and a half hearted muttering of prayer. This is the world of many Christians who slog away earning enough for the month with no savings or wriggle room if the car breaks down or central heating packs in. It is the pressure, grind and un-inspirational Monday to Friday that sucks us dry and lowers our horizons. The worries about office politics, decisions, targets and a hundred other concerns dominate our thoughts and cause us to be preoccupied. Then there are the weeks when everything explodes with a crisis at work or home and we are no use to anyone, never mind the Lord.

Spiritual disciplines don't make Monday to Friday pass more easily or more quickly. You are not going to find your job better paid or routes of promotion suddenly blossoming in front of you because you read your Bible every day for a week. I had a boss who was grumpy whether I read my Bible, prayed, fasted or did cartwheels, not that I fasted or did cartwheels I would have to admit. Your kids are still going to wake you at 3am and again at 4am and then stand at the side of the cot and want to play from sunrise. You can pray and wear sackcloth for a month and they will demand your last drop of energy. Sheriff Crone was still waiting for me down at Kilmarnock holding his clutch of pencils and staring down from the bench as I mumbled away in front of him as an out of town solicitor. Not much would change that scenario and make it pleasant. The targets will still be there, the concerns and pressures of work, the routines of home life and childcare will continue.

I have learned that perspective is everything when it comes to contentment and the vital key to it all is spiritual disciplines. They help ground us in what is actually the real world of eternal reality and help us cope with this tough but temporary life. They enable us to find joy, maturity, satisfaction and spiritual value in daily experiences. Without them we become spiritual Jekyll and Hyde characters. There is our Christian life and then there is all the other stuff.

What do I mean when I speak of spiritual disciplines? They are the things that you have heard preached many times and there is an obvious reason for that. If you have listened to a few sermons then I am certain you will have heard the preacher speak of the importance of reading the Bible and prayer. It isn't a quick or easy fix. It is not what most of us want to hear but it is true nonetheless. An ordinary life for God is not possible if we don't read the Bible and pray. You might get away with it if you bump along most of the time with an occasional good spell of usually self-righteous piety. I think we all know that is not the recipe for joy or contentment.

CHAPTER FOUR

The Bible

Read your Bible. It sounds easy, but if it were that easy we would all be doing it !! My first Bible was a dark red King James version with a zip. I have a strange memory of using it as a steering wheel in the back of my dad's car as we drove to visit our Gran each Sunday afternoon. I graduated to a Schofield Bible when I was 14 and I liked that Bible. It had footnotes and I did read some of the Bible using my trusty Schofield. I have a memory of standing at my bedroom window looking out to Dalmahoy Crescent reading 1 Corinthians through in one go when I was 16. I traded in my Schofield for a Newberry when I was 18 and I liked that even more. It was brown and although I didn't know how to use the grammatical sign system I felt grown up carrying it to church meetings. All of these Bibles were KJV and I still tend to think of verses in that translation due to the years of carrying these bibles and listening to preaching based upon that translation. I found the KJV version good for study but one of the reasons I managed to start reading the Bible regularly was that I got a New American Standard version and loved it right away. I could read easily and more intelligently. That doesn't sound too complicated and it wasn't, but in my experience it made a big difference. I still use a KJV from time to time and it resonates with me due to my upbringing but for reading the Bible I prefer a translation that is written in a language with which I am familiar and does not present an unnecessary linguistic obstacle.

I spend a lot of time studying and preparing sermons. I like finding shape and structure in the scriptures and seeing the truth unfold through study. I struggle with reading the Bible. I am not sure I really understand why that is so. I know that there is a spiritual battle going on and this is one key area of conflict so it is not going to be easy. My battle with the Bible is usually won or lost at the stage of lifting the book, sitting down and opening it. If I get past that mental hurdle then I read and enjoy. If I start thinking about a coffee, Facebook, the news, or any number of other things then my reading suffers.

I gave up on reading plans when they became an end in themselves and a box to tick at the end of the week. When I found myself cheating the plan and skipping bits to keep up I decided that it was not for me. I recognize that I am basically impatient and have to resist the thought that reading the Bible is an optional recreational activity and place it as a spiritual hygiene issue. It can't be relegated to something I do in my spare time.

What is the answer? It is neither pretty nor sophisticated but it has been effective for me: Read when you feel like it and read when you don't. Do you remember the old Nike slogan "Just do it"? I needed to get to the point where the objective ruled the subjective. What I knew in my head had to take over from how I felt. I know that reading the Bible calibrates me for the day. I don't suddenly become wise and spiritual but my mind is set in the right direction. I know it is spiritual food and that without it I will be weaker that day. Temptations will be stronger; my resolve will be feeble, my decision-making will be less God conscious and if I continue to neglect the Bible I know that I will lose perspective in relation to the issues I will face during these days. I know all of these things therefore I have to read whether I feel like it or not. I have to prioritise what I know over how I feel.

I need to read the Bible when I enjoy it and when I don't. That simple thought has helped me as I no longer have the expectation that every time I read it is going to be a significant spiritual experience. What I read may stay in my mind or shed some light on a particular problem. My emotions may be stirred as I begin or end the day. These things have happened but I don't expect them to happen every time I lift my Bible. I have learned that a realistic approach to regular reading produces a sustainable routine that meets reasonable expectations. I have found that short but regular reading is better than sporadic catch up guilt trips.

When you look back into the Old Testament you see that the Word of God had an important place in the national and family life of the children of Israel.

"Hear, O Israel: The LORD our God, the LORD is one!
"You shall love the LORD your God with all your heart, with all your soul, and with all your strength.
"And these words which I command you today shall be in your heart.
"You shall teach them diligently to your children, and shall talk of them when you sit in your house, when you walk by the way, when you lie down, and when you rise up.

"You shall bind them as a sign on your hand, and they shall be as frontlets between your eyes.
"You shall write them on the doorposts of your house and on your gates".
(Deuteronomy 6:4-9)

What about us in the 21st Century, with all our Bible apps, reading plans, translations and study Bibles? These things are all just tools and can end up being a distraction as we play about with the app or stress about the reading plan. When you strip it all back you should get a translation of the Bible which you can read comfortably. Find an app that suits and stick to it or, as in my case, avoid the apps, iPad and online stuff and hold a Bible in your hands. If that is what you do, try sticking to the same Bible and it will become like a familiar friend. You will know where you are with it and you will find it easier to pick it up. There is no right or wrong in this, just use whatever causes you to sit down, take a breath and read.

Read until you have to do something else or your mind wanders. Try and read without putting pressure on yourself by setting a time or a set passage, just read. I can only tell you what I do and it may help someone. I read until my mind begins to wander or my eyes want to close and I stop, close my eyes for a bit and pray about what I have read. I then read a little more and repeat the process. I don't read long sections of scripture but find it is better for me to read a little and stop, pray, think and repeat that short process a few times. That may work for you and it may not. The point is that you need to find a process that enables you to read and let the scriptures sink in below the surface before the day blows them out of your mind.

I also think it helps to see the daily reading of the Bible as part of your routine. You brush your teeth whether you can be bothered or not. You wouldn't leave the house without doing that because it is so familiar and you know it is necessary. The day is not going to go well if your breath and teeth are advertising what you had for your dinner last night. It is the desire to look after your teeth as well as the effect that would have on others that makes you clean them every day without fail. Hygiene issues are important to most of us so we build the teeth brushing time into our routine before the day begins. Breakfast can be adapted for the time we have, as can the hair and other rituals but teeth brushing is non negotiable.

Reading the Bible is a spiritual health and hygiene issue. If I occasionally miss out on reading the Bible it is not something that is obvious to others. Like the teeth thing, the closer you are to someone then the more obvious it is that something has been missed. When you regularly miss out on the Bible then it becomes glaringly obvious to others. It can be seen in your character and conduct. I know in my own family that my fleshly character rears its ugly head on those days and I can also spot it in those closest to me. There is a change of tone in the way we speak and a hard attitude to others when we are not reading our Bibles.

There are other thoughts that hinder me from time to time. I am looking at pages which I have read before. I know the stories and have preached them or told them to children on many occasions. I am not reading something new but am going over old ground. Negative thoughts come into my head as my hands open the lovely soft cover of my

NASB Bible. I also struggle because I tend to forget what I have read within minutes and wonder if it is worthwhile spending the time if I am just going through a sort of ritual to make me feel better. There can be a lot of negativity in this area of conflict; I don't have time, I have read this before, I will do it later, I have so much to do, I will catch up another day ... does any of this sound familiar?

I want to highlight three reasons for reading the Bible on a daily basis (in no particular order). These are far from exhaustive but I have found them to be important. I recently heard a quote which I think was by John MacArthur, "the word of Christ in your heart and in your mind is the handle by which the Holy Spirit turns your will". These words have stuck in my mind as they make sense to me. Reading the Bible every day changes me. The Holy Spirit uses the Word of God to shape us and form Christlikeness in our character. This is not a short term project and requires consistent reading and submission to the Word. "Let the word of Christ dwell in you richly in all wisdom" (Colossians 3:16).

Crisis Management

The spiritual conflict in which we are engaged is described in Ephesians Ch6. The weapon at our disposal is the sword of the Spirit, which is the Word of God. Bible scholars will tell you that this refers to the spoken word, not the written word. It doesn't refer to the concept of the Bible as a sword. I don't know how widespread the practice is among those who teach children at Sunday school or Bible Clubs but we used to love the sword drill. I can remember it in the old Hope Hall, a corrugated iron hall on the Main Street in Bridge of Weir. Willie Taylor was in charge and he issued the instructions, "Sheathe your swords". A frantic movement of our Bibles followed as we placed them under our arms. We tried to cheat as young boys do and held our fingers in pages. "Draw your swords", and out they came as we held them above our heads and listened to the verse being called out from the front and then we waited .... "Go" and we were off, frantically searching for our verse and standing up when we got it. It was a great activity but is not the thought in Ephesians Ch6.

When we need it, the Spirit of God will bring the appropriate verse or section of the scriptures to our minds. This is the spoken Word of God referred to as the Sword of the Spirit. We have to have read and taken in the written Word before the Spirit can bring it to the forefront of our minds. Remember when Satan tempted the Lord in the wilderness and was defeated by the quotation of scripture as the Lord wielded the sword of the Spirit. It wasn't all or any scriptures that He used, they were relevant to the temptation.

I can clearly remember a day when the Spirit of God brought the Word of God to bear upon me in difficult circumstances. My employment was pretty secure, or so I thought. I worked for a city centre legal firm that had blue chip clients. I remember the day my world changed. We lost our biggest client overnight and when I arrived for work that day I knew there was a problem. The redundancy process began and the meeting with the partners passed in a blur. In what seemed a very short time I was left sitting in my office staring at the wall wondering what I was going to say to Sharon. Before I lifted the phone and made some calls for another job a couple of verses came into my mind which I had not thought about for years. "Trust in the LORD with all your heart, And lean not on your own understanding; In all your ways acknowledge Him, And He shall direct your paths" (Proverbs 3:5, 6). That text had hung in my parent's house over the piano in the living room throughout my childhood. The framed text was part of the house and family life but I had been away from the house since I was 17 years old and hadn't thought about that text since. It was the right scripture for the moment and I still remember the sense of peace and the pressure lifting as I committed the issues of that day to the Lord. It was one of the crisis days of my life and the Spirit swung His sword to slay the fears which were gripping me.

The Bible

There are times when it seems that Satan has targeted you for some special attention. He comes at you with his customary subtlety: an angel of light, a roaring lion, whatever it takes. It is in these times of doubt that you can crumble. Peter was brave when he stood facing armed men but somehow the voice of a girl by a fire got to him and his courage failed. His denial of the Lord was a necessary life lesson that the Lord allowed him to experience. The Lord had prayed for him that his faith would not fail, and it didn't, but Peter knew the bitterness of failure. It was a taste that never left his mouth. The big, bold leader of men was reduced to a shamed, weeping sinner. I have been there and done the same thing as Peter. All alone in the big world of work I have sat quiet when I should have spoken and laughed when I should have excused myself. I too have felt ashamed. In the heat of that particular battle the Sword of the Spirit can make the difference between disaster and recovery.

A few years ago I had the strange experience of going to a school reunion. I think it must have been 15 years since I had left school and seen most of my old classmates. It was a fascinating experience for all sorts of reasons. Everyone was a success and life was good. The superficial conversation flowed and people pretended and told their stories. Everyone was having a good time. That evening disturbed me more than I initially realised. By that time I was no longer a solicitor and was a Gospel preacher and Bible teacher, not the most glamorous of vocations. I lived in the same village in which we had all grown up and was the only one of the group still in the locality. I was married with kids and again was only one of two people married and with children. It began to needle me that perhaps I was missing out on something. I had no career, company car or business trips and lived in a modest house with an ordinary life. I was in the early stages of Psalm 73. That Psalm helped me greatly as did a verse from Psalm 16 "But to the saints that are in the earth, and to the excellent, in whom is all my delight" (Psalms 16:3). I had been reading these psalms around the time of that reunion and the Spirit took that Sword and slew the doubts and covetousness. He recalibrated my thinking and gave me perspective and a fresh appreciation of what is important. "Your word I have hidden in my heart, That I might not sin against You!" (Psalms 119:11).

Shaping Character

I read a blog by Jon Bloom on the Desiring God web site entitled "Six Benefits of Ordinary Daily Devotions". It was a good post and worth finding if it is still online. I want to quote his summary at the end of that post, "Brick upon brick a building is built. Lesson upon lesson a degree is earned. Stroke upon stroke a painting is created. Your devotions may have seemed ordinary today, but God is making something extraordinary through it. Press on. Don't short-change the process".

Perhaps the least dramatic reason for reading the Bible every day is the long term effect it has upon you. The Spirit of God shapes and changes our character as we regularly fill our minds with the Truth of God. He doesn't make us a slightly better version of who we are, He changes us.

The day I typed this I was reminded that I am getting on a bit. I received a text from my son, which said "osm"; I didn't have a clue what he was saying and so had no option but to demonstrate my ignorance and ask the question. I got an answer that was obvious the moment I saw it (osm = awesome) but still showed me that I do not think in phonetic acronyms. I still punctuate my texts !!! There was a time when WWJD was the current "thing" among Christians. It appeared on every conceivable object from bracelets to bumper stickers and I think was only downgraded when Jabez's prayer took over. WWJD is actually a good tag line for life. What would Jesus do? (Perhaps a more pertinent question to ask is, What would Jesus want me to do?) How do I know the answer to that? Reading the Bible is the only means to that end. Daily reading will cause me to think differently. My thinking will be more in tune with God than with the world in which I live. The Word of God will shape my priorities. My love for Christ will impact me during the week and not just for an hour on Sunday morning. When issues arise for which there is no chapter and verse I will have learned principles and formed convictions enabling me to make decisions that are consistent with the name of the Lord Jesus Christ.

Let me encourage you in your ordinary life to read the Bible.

CHAPTER FIVE

Prayer

If ever there is an area of Christian living about which I have preached and felt the hypocrisy of my words it is prayer. I can't remember where I heard it but someone said that this is the area of life, which Christians talk about so much, and practise so little.

Sermons abound about the prayer lives of Daniel, Jacob, Abraham, Moses, Paul and even the Lord Jesus. There are probably more promises made and broken in relation to prayer than any other aspect of living as a Christian. How often have I promised, "I will pray for you", and failed to do so.

Why is prayer such a battle? As I thought about this it occurred to me that prayer is where the spiritual realities of my life function in their purest sense. Regular personal prayer is a private experience and therefore has no attraction to the flesh. The same can't be said for ticking boxes in Bible reading plans and studying the scriptures. There is plenty for the flesh to work on in these areas. It may also be that Satan is aware of the power in prayer and we are not. He may target our prayer lives in order to weaken our Christian experience. If he stops us from praying then he deprives us of the power that scripture promises is available through prayer.

Prayer also brings me into the quietness of God's presence and I find myself face to face with the purity of light that characterises God and exposes my true spiritual condition. I know that if I am intent on sinning in one way or another then I cannot bring myself to spend time in prayer. I know that if I have outstanding issues with another person then I cannot spend time in prayer. In these moments I need a lesser light to shine around me rather than the piercing shaft of Divine brilliance which shows me up "warts and all". I choose any number of lesser lights such as Christian company and conversation, which may be good but is not God. Think of Moses in Exodus Chapter 3 standing before the unquenchable fire of God's presence. It is an uncomfortable place when God is present and speaking to us. I heard a sermon which had as one of the inevitable three points a powerful statement, "Moses had to experience the trauma of God's presence". It was there that he heard God say "I am who I am" and had experience with God with no one else present, just like prayer ought to be.

I want to focus our attention on three problems I have encountered in my own thinking in relation to prayer. It is not easy to admit having a stop start or non-existent prayer life and as with all of these things, taking the time to examine why is a good place to start when seeking a change for the better.

Prayer is time consuming

It is amazing how we never have time to do things that we consider unimportant. Things that don't matter to us get put on the back burner and consigned to the pending tray of our lives. They sit in the part of our planner which is reserved for things that would be good to do but not essential for today.

Prayer takes time and time is a precious commodity. I have to remind myself of the importance of God and the necessity of speaking to Him, never mind the privilege, otherwise I will never make time to pray. I know that prayer is starting to slip in my thinking when I begin to fit it in as an afterthought, usually in the car. I am falling into the trap of thinking that prayer is something that can be done while I am doing something else, as some kind of multitasking activity. By doing this and thinking this way I am trying to redeem some down time rather than allocating some quality time.

I remember reading a good book called "Too busy not to pray" by Bill Hybels. It is a small book but it changed the way I thought about prayer. I took a lot from that book, including the ACTS structure of personal prayer: Adoration, Confession, Thanksgiving and Supplication. Little helpful hints like that can make a difference. I have proved the truth of the title of that little book over and over again. How often have I rushed into the day with so much to be done and no time to spare? My mind focused on tasks and ignoring the Lord with all His resources and peace to impart if I would sit still in His presence for a few moments before the day begins. Prayer is time well spent and never wasted.

Prayer is repetitive

Saying the same things to God can easily become saying

prayers rather than praying. I can remember when it was my turn to say the grace at our dinner table when I was young. "God bless this food and make me good for Jesus sake, Amen". Prayers for children at the side of the bed tend to be a recitation of a list to God and sometimes our prayers can become just like that. We go through a list and mention names like reading a phone book. Is that really what prayer should be?

I was returning home from Indonesia on an Emirates flight through Dubai when I witnessed the prayers of a Muslim man. He was sitting next to me and got up and went over to the galley area of the plane and knelt down. He was praying and although I had no idea what he was saying I did notice the repetitive nature of his prayers. This was evidently an unbreakable habit of life for this man and sufficiently important to him that not even the confines of a plane would restrict him. It struck me that if he could overhear my prayers then they may seem equally repetitive. Although it may on the surface appear to be a noble thing to have such unbreakable habits of devotion I concluded that I should never view my prayers in the same way as that man did. I did not want to have a form of prayers that required repetitive chanting as if the expression of those words had value due to their repetition. I also did not want to see prayer as a duty to be performed giving value to the process rather than the content of prayer. I know it is out of context but the truth is equally applicable, "a few words with the understanding" rather than a multitude of words without understanding ought to be our aim in prayer.

Say what you mean and mean what you say.

Prayer seems pointless

Stuff happens whether you pray or don't pray. I mean isn't God in control and working out His own purpose and hasn't the story been written and is just being enacted? These thoughts come from time to time. Does praying make any difference? Are my days any different if I don't pray? Is the difference in my sense of wellbeing or is it more meaningful than that? Does prayer only make me feel good?

These points make their presence felt in my thinking from time to time and I have never been able to completely eradicate them from mind, hence they pop up when least welcome. In this issue more than another aspect of our lives for God we are dependent upon the Word of God as prayer is not something which can be properly measured in our tangible, material world. Without scripture we simply can't tell whether prayer works. We are only able to experience one side of the conversation and don't have access to anything more than what leaves our heart and is articulated in prayer. We have to accept what God says about prayer in His Word and so it becomes a matter of faith.

The prayers that we are considering are the routine, regular daily prayers of an ordinary life. It is not Nehemiah standing before the King in a moment of crisis or Elijah asking God to bring drought into the land and by so doing fulfil His promise. It is not even the Lord spending all night in prayer prior to choosing his disciples. I am thinking of the prayers of Daniel and his routine of praying three times a day. It is the prayers to which Paul refers so often in his writings as he encourages various believers by telling them that they feature regularly in his prayers. Paul was not always witnessing before authorities and forging across lands with the gospel. He spent a considerable part of his service for God in prison and at places such as Ephesus where he led a fairly ordinary life teaching the local church and holding down a job.

There is a fair amount of instruction and encouragement in scripture for routine prayer. Paul often exhorted his readers to pray regularly and gave guidance by including his own prayers in his letters. By including those prayers in his epistles he left us an insight into the content of his prayers and there is so much for us to learn by reading his prayers. He told them how often he prayed for them and then asked them to pray for him in return. He referred to prayer in relation to his release from imprisonment when writing to Philemon. As he thought about the need for the young churches to grow in their knowledge of God he committed the issue to the Lord by prayer. Whether it was for the restoration of communion with the Lord after sin had brought defilement, a cure for the anxiety caused by life's troubles or the necessary encouragement to keep going in the Christian pathway, the writers of the New Testament all point us to the necessity of prayer.

When considering the place of prayer in your busy life, take into account the example of the Lord Jesus who regularly prayed. Don't forget the exhortations of the New Testament Epistles to pray and not to give up. Don't model your prayers on the repetitive and powerless prayers that you may hear but rather read the prayers of the Bible and absorb the reality of David's Psalms, Jeremiah's anguish,

Moses's intercession, Elijah's pleas and of course the intimacy of the Lord in John Ch17. Trust the Word of God in relation to the effect of prayer in your circumstances and others for whom you pray.

Perhaps the most significance aspect of prayer to consider is the impact it has upon yourself. There is a feel good factor when you are praying regularly which may be as much about the flesh as anything. However there is a genuine impact upon our spiritual wellbeing and relationship with the Lord when we pray. I think most of us know that we live better and sin less when we pray regularly. Our love for the Lord and His people is greatest when we are on our knees on a daily basis worshipping and praying for others. Our resistance against temptation and our attitude to others is so much better when we start the day with God. That is surely reason enough to make time to pray!

There are many Psalms which can help us to pray. I am going to comment on a couple but this is just a taste of a large resource brought to us by God from the experiences of men who wrestled with the same problems which we have and spoke to the same God.

It is good to give thanks to the LORD, And to sing praises to Your name, O Most High;
To declare Your lovingkindness in the morning, And Your faithfulness every night,
(Psalms 92:1, 2).

The Psalmist teaches us the value of focusing in our morning prayers upon the lovingkindess of God. As we anticipate the day with whatever lies ahead we should take time to remember and give thanks to the Lord for His loyal love and goodness. Whatever happens in the day we can call to mind His intrinsic goodness and love to us.

In the evening the Psalmist is encouraging us to give thanks for the Lord's faithfulness. We are able to look back over the hours that have passed into eternity and trace the faithfulness of God. He didn't forsake us, He did keep His Word and His faithfulness is truly great.

Give ear to my words, O LORD, Consider my meditation.
Give heed to the voice of my cry, My King and my God, For to You I will pray.
My voice You shall hear in the morning, O LORD; In the morning I will direct it to You, And I will look up.
(Psalms 5:1-3).

In Psalm 5 we learn about taking refuge in the Lord when we are under attack. The scripture does teach us that the Lord is our refuge but what does that mean in practical daily experience. When you read Psalm 5 you get a good idea of what that would look like on a Monday morning.

When David was under attack he took his complaint to the Lord in prayer. His prayer was marked by honesty and was the honest groan of a man in great need. There is no hiding his true need in the Lord's presence. As he prayed he personally addressed God as his King even although David was a King himself. He prayed persistently and twice over said that he would pray in the morning. It seems that the first thought David had on waking was about his problems and difficulties and that is very often the way it is with us. Instead of scheming and planning David took these worries and turned them into prayers. Most of us wake up and within minutes are thinking about issues and problems which we will have to face that day. People, exams, contracts, schedules, travel, whatever it may be. That is not going to change but the question is what do we do with these thoughts and anxieties that grip us so early in the day?

David also wrote of his systematic approach to daily prayer. He said "In the morning I will order my prayer to You." This was an expression which was used of priests as they ordered the sacrifice on the altar or arranged the showbread on the table in the Tabernacle. David was not haphazard and gave thought to a system. He organised his daily prayers. Sometimes my prayers are like a memory test. I mention what I can remember and that is one sure way for stuff to fall off the prayer radar.

I love David's confidence in God. He eagerly watched for the answer to his prayers. He didn't see prayer as words expressed and lost into the air. He had communicated with His God and King and looked for an answer. He used the same word that Habakkuk used (2:1) "I will stand on my guard post and station myself on the rampart; and I will keep watch to see what He will speak to me, and how I may reply when I am reproved." The picture is of a guard at his military post waiting for the messenger that he has sent to return. I wonder if I expect God to respond one way or the other to what I say to Him.

These are only two of many Psalms which record the experiences of the Psalmists with God. There is so much that we can learn about prayer from these sections of scripture and I would encourage you to read them and put these and many other lessons you will learn into practice.

Let me encourage you in your ordinary life to pray every day.

CHAPTER SIX

A Quiet Life

"Aspire to lead a quiet life", easier said than done when you are in a church which seems to be anything but peaceful and quiet. The Thessalonians had a lot going on. They were having a hard time from people in their community. They had anxiety about recent bereavements and different views about whether they should keep working while they waited for the Lord's return. I imagine there were excitable people among them who spoke with great passion and narrow focus about these matters and then there would be others who were a bit "dour", as we say in Scotland. They had all experienced a remarkable transformation as they "turned to God from idols to serve the living and true God, and to wait for His Son from heaven, whom He raised from the dead, even Jesus who delivers us from the wrath to come" (1 Thessalonians 1:9, 10). In the midst of great suffering their reputation for faith and love had spread throughout the region. Any church of any age would be delighted to possess their reputation. It was exciting and dangerous days for the Thessalonian church. A quiet life would be rare.

Paul had been concerned about them since he was forced to leave Thessalonica and had sent Timothy to check on their progress and encourage them in their suffering. What would he write to such a church? Should they make a stand against the persecution? Should they be encouraged to be bold and do great deeds to emulate the Old Testament heroes of faith? Would Paul stir them to martyrdom?

It is probably no surprise that Paul exhorts them in aspirational terms not to rest on their reputation or past achievements. He has praised them for what they have been doing but wants them to be ambitious rather than content with their progress. Having said that, I think that Paul's desire for the Thessalonians is on a different trajectory to a lot of what we see and hear among Christian churches today. In our age of social media there is a tendency to want to show off and gain popularity or notoriety. Numbers and stats seem to be all important. Visibility is everything and it is usually all about books sales, twitter followers or funding. Ordinary is not exceptional and quiet doesn't get you noticed.

Paul's exhortation is not exactly the sort of rallying call you get at a Passion Conference, Resurgence live stream or funding grab. There aren't a lot of writers on book tours with this message. If you listen to headline speakers at big Christian conferences, it is all about empowering a generation to do spectacular things for God. The reality is that they won't because they can't and there is no expectation from scripture that they should. Once the excitement of the event dies away, you are back to the reality of paying the bills, sitting exams, cleaning the bathroom, looking after the kids and taking care of business. Experiencing awe inspiring, spine tingling preaching and hearing all the stories of "blessing" from guys who are bouncing around in their own stratosphere of ecstatic experience is counter productive for the majority of us mere mortals. It simply does not equate to the routine ordinariness of our lives. Before you know where you are you have spent a morning at work and are sitting at a desk rather than floating on cloud nine. The rent remains due and the fuel bills don't disappear because you have been inspired to do "great things" for God. For you and me the "great thing" would be paying the bills by working hard and honestly just as the Lord Jesus did until he was 30 years old. If you are not careful you end up living the majority of your life as a parenthesis to the weekends, which you believe is the spiritual part of your life.

Paul didn't incite them to make a big noise in their community or get noticed, which is really interesting and is a different message from the radical missional messages packaged so effectively to young, sincere Christians in the joy of first love. In fact, he was saying the opposite. Paul is calming the Thessalonians and trying to avoid them losing touch with the day to day realities of life. Fixating on the Lord's return could lead them to living in an unsustainable and debilitating state of anticipation. It seems that he doesn't want them to get carried away, become radical or hit the headlines. He isn't asking them to be restless.

Hiebert comments that this exhortation..."implies that there was a spirit of restlessness in the young church. It was due, apparently, not to political influences, but rather to the new religious experiences and hopes that had gripped their minds. Although there is nothing to prove that this restlessness was caused by their excited anticipation of the impending return of Christ, such a connection, nevertheless, seems probable. The inspiring expectation of Christ's return, whereby earthly interests were reduced in importance in their eyes, had become the centre of their excited interest. This connection seems justified from the fact that Paul immediately follows this exhortation with his treatment of the second advent, thereupon to return to further practical exhortations concerning daily living. Paul urges that this "eschatological restlessness" be turned into the proper channel. Instead of allowing their excited expectation to lead them to neglect their daily duties, let them use this enthusiasm faithfully to fulfil those duties". (Hiebert, D. Edmond: 1 & 2 Thessalonians: BMH Book. 1996)

Paul wrote in similar terms to Timothy. "I exhort first of all that supplications, prayers, intercessions, and giving of thanks be made for all men, for kings and all who are in authority, that we may lead a quiet and peaceable life in all godliness and reverence.
(1 Timothy 2:1, 2).

On the face of it, the exhortation to be ambitious to lead a quiet life does seem to be counterintuitive. Ambition is often displayed in an eagerness to achieve, to progress and accomplish great things. It drives a person on, creating dissatisfaction with present circumstances and a longing after future possibilities. It can have a negative connotation due to the objective of ambition and the means employed to obtain whatever it may be. It can dominate a person at the expense of others and lead to a distortion of their character and damage to their reputation. According to Robertson's Word Pictures, the word means, "to act from love of honour, to be ambitious in the good sense. The Latin 'ambitio' has a bad sense from 'ambire', to go both ways to gain one's point".

As with most words in the Bible, context is king. Paul is not speaking of an overwhelmingly selfish desire to accomplish great things for the sake of our own glory. In that context Jeremiah records a warning given by the Lord to Baruch the son of Neriah, "And do you seek great things for yourself? Do not seek them" (Jeremiah 45:5). Paul wrote similar words to the Romans "Be of the same mind toward one another. Do not set your mind on high things, but associate with the humble. Do not be wise in your own opinion" (Romans 12:16).

Strive to lead a quiet life. It just seems strange to put the two ideas side by side. Surely if we do nothing as Christians we will have a quiet life? It doesn't require any effort on our part to merge into the background of our community and be invisible. If we do nothing for God and are nothing for God then we will never raise our heads above the trench wall and get noticed by the enemy. Does Paul mean that we have to be spiritually inert? What about storming the gates of hell and pulling down strongholds? What about doing hard things and facing our giants? What does Paul mean by a quiet life?

In typical preaching fashion let's consider what a quiet life is not.

A quiet life is not an isolated life. Paul doesn't want the Thessalonians to shut themselves off from the city and have no contact with people. He is not advocating, nor did he live, a monastic life. Some of us consider a quiet life to be one of stress free isolation from people and problems like Charles Dickens wrote in the Pickwick Papers "Anything for a quiet life, as the man said when he took the situation at the lighthouse." We don't get too close to others as it will bring hassle and commitment. We want to be selfish and spend our time on our family and ourselves. We don't want to be busy serving God or loving others. We would rather be in a lighthouse of our own construction, protected against any disturbance and at a distance from others. The Thessalonians hadn't been living isolated lives and Paul wasn't about to start telling them to withdraw from their relationships and stop loving their brothers and sisters in Christ, never mind the people of the city.

Being in relationship with others is good and being alone is not as good. That is why Adam got Eve. Although sin had not yet appeared in the Genesis narrative the Lord saw that it was not good for Adam to be alone and made a companion for him to share his life of service. God made marriage, family, nations and the church which are all based upon people being in active relationship with each other. I have known some people who want a quiet life because they can't be bothered with the effort of maintaining relationships and are plain lazy. Isolation mitigates against most Biblical instruction for our lives with one example being the instruction in Hebrews to make it your business not to be absent when the church meets, "And let us consider one another in order to stir up love and good works, not forsaking the assembling of ourselves together, as is the manner of some, but exhorting one another, and so much the more as you see the Day approaching."(Hebrews 10:24, 25). It is hard to love and serve each other if we live at a distance from each other.

A quiet life is also not a careless life. Think of world missions. I have sat and listened to appeals for young men and women to leave their homes and travel abroad to serve the Lord. In Scotland there is an added appeal of joining your name to the long and distinguished list of missionaries from here who left their home comforts and served the Lord in Africa and other far flung parts of the world. Who would not be impressed by the stories of David Livingstone, Dan Crawford, Mary Slessor and many others from the more recent past who gave so much and experienced such hardship to bring the Gospel to the unreached people of our world. The reality is that 99.9% of Christians will not go abroad to serve the Lord as missionaries with perhaps some spending a gap year at a Christian school or orphanage. We are not going to be camping in the Angolan bush, cutting our way through the Borneo jungle or climbing the mountains of Nepal. Does that mean that we shouldn't care about the unreached people of our world? Of course not! You either give or go, but an ordinary life for God will mean that wherever you are, with whatever resources you have, you care about others who have not heard the Gospel. I find it interesting that in our day of incredible communication there seems to be a diminishing interest in mission work. Is it not the case that churches of a previous generation in mining, fishing and agricultural communities comprised of men and women who never set foot out of Scotland yet had a deep and generous interest in mission work? They had ordinary lives but they had a heart for the Gospel at home and abroad.

Paul had commended the Thessalonians for their love for people beyond their city, "but concerning brotherly love you have no need that I should write to you, for you yourselves are taught by God to love one another; and indeed you do so toward all the brethren who are in all Macedonia. But we urge you, brethren, that you increase more and more" (1 Thessalonians 4:9, 10). They were a caring church and a quiet life would not stop them from loving their fellow Christians throughout Macedonia. They were not like Paul who travelled extensively throughout the region yet they had a love for the Christians in their region. Paul wanted them to increase their love and live quietly. It wasn't one at the expense of the other. A quiet life does not mean a careless life.

So then, what is a quiet life?

The word Paul used and is translated as "quiet" means to be silent. It appears in Luke's Gospel, "And Jesus, answering, spoke to the lawyers and Pharisees, saying, "Is it lawful to heal on the Sabbath?" But they kept silent. And He took him and healed him, and let him go". (Luke 14:3, 4). In the context of the Lord's return, Paul is instructing the Thessalonians to lead peaceful lives, free of conflict and hostility toward others. Keep under the radar and don't make a lot of noise. Don't attract trouble and don't make a fuss in your community.

Was he being hypocritical? After all you could hardly accuse Paul of being quiet when he went into Thessalonica with the Gospel. He was in the synagogue for three Sabbath days and the result was that the city was in an uproar with Jason taken hostage and Paul having to leave in a hurry. Not what you might call a quiet life! I think we make a mistake if we assume that Paul's life was a constant round of very exciting and dangerous encounters with violence and opposition. There is no doubt that he had more than his fair share of persecution and suffering which he recounts in 2 Corinthians ch11. He was breaking new ground with the Gospel and experiencing prejudice and hostility as a stranger with a strange message.

He was also the object of opposition from his former friends and colleagues as a traitor to the Jewish nation. Don't forget that he spent months and years in locations teaching and working with churches without any recorded flare ups and conflict. His life was not the model for the people who received his letters who were based in one community establishing a local church and living for God among unbelieving friends, family and workmates. His circumstances were not to be coveted although his example of godliness and integrity within his circumstances were worthy of following. He did not want the believers at Thessalonica to be in prison, protesting against Roman authorities or constantly provoking their community. He wanted the church at Thessalonica to flourish, characterised by Christlikeness in their sexual purity, love for each other and quiet, dignified, hardworking, ordinary lives.

How can we strive for this quiet life?

Many of us have periods of quietness in our lives. We

don't seek them but are glad enough when they come along. They are like a calm in the midst of the storm of our otherwise frantic existences. The problem is that we are often not content with such quietness, if it continues for a while. It gets boring and uneventful. We miss the drama of living in a state of crisis. We don't know what to worry or complain about. This is the area to focus on if you want to strive for a quiet life. Without contentment we may have periods of quietness in our lives but they won't last. Pride, curiosity, boredom, selfishness and many other unattractive aspects of our flesh will rear their head and soon the quiet life is a fond memory. Humility is a close relation of contentment and both are the guardians of a quiet life. For a quiet life to be more than an occasional, if much talked about and fondly remembered oasis of calm, we need to seek contentment like a garden entered through the gate of humility.

Andrew Murray wrote a book entitled "Humility" which I recommend anyone to read. He directs you to the importance of humility and defines it as "not a something which we bring to God, or he bestows; it is simply the sense of entire nothingness, which comes when we see how truly God is all, and in which we make way for God to be all. When the creature realizes that this is the true nobility, and consents to be with his will, his mind, his affections, the form, the vessel in which the life and glory of God are to work and manifest themselves, he sees that humility is simply acknowledging his position as creature, and yielding to God His place".

Perhaps the most telling section of his book is found in the chapter dealing with humility in daily life. He writes, "the insignificancies of daily life are the importances and the tests of eternity, because they prove what really is the spirit that possesses us." I think that Murray has it spot on and is right to identity the ordinary things of life as the areas in which our true spiritual condition is found. You don't have to be humble to be ordinary but you do have to be humble to be content with an ordinary life. If we accept Murray's definition we can see that a quiet life is possible when we lose any big ideas we have about ourselves and yield to God.

In the everyday matters of life we need to see ourselves as not only living for God but God living in and through us. The small, regular and non-spectacular matters of Monday to Friday take on a different significance. It is in these things we prove our God, it is in these things that we please our God, it is in these things that we worship our God. God is truly glorified in us on a Tuesday morning when we read our Bible and pray, give up our seat on the train, smile and say "thank you" when we get our coffee, focus on our work and do our best, avoid the gossip and refrain from undermining our boss in front of his boss, don't click on the spam link in our e-mail, give thanks to God before we eat our lunch in the company cafeteria, stay until 5pm when no-one else is around and so it goes on. It is a quiet life but it is also a good life since it the life that God has for us.

We may think of the humble person as the proverbial Caspar Milquetoast, a character invented by the cartoonist H T Webster in 1924 in a New York paper series called "The timid soul". Webster described him as the man who speaks softly and gets hit with a big stick. That may still be the perception of a humble man held by some but it is not what the Bible presents as humility. The truly humble person is not weak, in fact it is the very opposite. It takes courage and strength to live humbly. It requires you to swim against the tide of modern psychology which emphasises and aggressively promotes self and self-esteem.

I had a look at Wikipedia, that fount of information, to see what it said about self-esteem. "In the mid-1960s, Morris Rosenberg and social-learning theorists defined self-esteem as a personal worth or worthiness. Nathaniel Branden in 1969 defined self-esteem as "the experience of being competent to cope with the basic challenges of life and being worthy of happiness." According to Branden, self-esteem is the sum of (a feeling of personal capacity) and self-respect (a feeling of personal worth). It exists as a consequence of the implicit judgment that every person has of their ability to face life's challenges, to understand and solve problems, and their right to achieve, and be given respect". I have no idea as to the veracity of these quotations since I have no informed notion of psychology but at face value they represent a view of self which is not Biblical and does not produce true humility.

There is strong pressure in our world to look within ourselves and discover the potential that exists. We are told to see ourselves as having no boundaries, no limits, nothing that will stop us fulfilling our potential other than a lack of self belief. For a Western world that treats faith in God as something for the simple minded there is a tremendous push for us to have faith in ourselves. If you want to lose weight, just believe. If you want to be Shamu's new trainer at Seaworld, just believe. If you want to win the latest tacky talent contest, just believe. Contestants speak about their life being complete if they can just win, all they need to do is believe and they will accomplish what they want so badly.

Strong faith is promoted as an essential ingredient to success but it is faith in self and not God. This is idolatry and leads to terrible pride and envy. It is also very different to the teaching of the Bible. When we depend on ourselves and live independently from God we are putting ourselves in the place that God ought to occupy in our hearts. We serve ourselves, please ourselves, rely on our resources, praise ourselves and seek glory and praise from others. We worship at the altar of ME. "Just believe", "have faith", "stay strong" are all expressions which point us away from God and toward ourselves.

If we are honest when we look within there is not limitless potential and there are few amazing attributes just waiting to be unleashed on an unsuspecting world. There is wickedness, corruption and inevitable failure. The Bible tells us in no uncertain terms that sin is ugly and seems to be at its most ugly within the human frame. "As it is written: "There is none righteous, no, not one; There is none who understands; There is none who seeks after God. They have all turned aside; They have together become unprofitable; There is none who does good, no, not one." Their throat is an open tomb; With their tongues they have practised deceit"; "The poison of asps is under their lips"; "Whose mouth is full of cursing and bitterness." "Their feet are swift to shed blood; Destruction and misery are in their ways; And the way of peace they have not known."

"There is no fear of God before their eyes"(Romans 3:10-18). It is not exactly a delightful picture.

We are created in the image and likeness of God but as fallen human beings we are not as wonderful or amazing as we perhaps think we are and when we start to believe otherwise we are in big trouble. A realistic understanding of our sin should ensure that the last thing we should be striving for is self-actualisation. Taking the sin that is in our hearts and giving it full expression is a recipe for disaster. No one should see a full blown version of the nasty, spiteful, jealous, selfish and downright wicked person that I am at the core of my being. And I am sorry to tell you I have no desire to see a full manifestation or actualisation of your flesh either. There should be as little of self on display as possible, whether actualised, realised or whatever the current term is for the worship of ego.

The blessedness of becoming a Christian is that our sins are forgiven and we become a new creation in Christ Jesus. Our old man has died and will never live again. We are essentially and organically new people after our conversion. We are born again into the family of God and indwelt by the Holy Spirit. We live different lives evidenced in our obedience to the Word of God and love for our Lord Jesus. We breathe the atmosphere of grace and are kept secure for heaven by God's unbreakable promise. It is a truly wonderful and eternal transformation when you are saved, redeemed, forgiven and restored to God. Having said all of that, until the Lord returns and we experience the transformation of our bodies to what the Bible calls our bodies of glory (Philippians 3:21), we are still incarcerated in the body that is described as our body of humiliation. It is the sphere in which we daily battle against sin and temptation. One of the greatest problems we face is the sin of pride leading to discontentment. So we have to stand beside the Apostle Paul and say, "But God forbid that I should glory, save in the cross of our Lord Jesus Christ, by whom the world is crucified unto me, and I unto the world" (Galatians 6:14). When we stand in the shadow of the cross and gaze upon that thorn scarred brow and those nail pierced hands and feet we must humble ourselves and by so doing be content.

"Therefore we also, since we are surrounded by so great a cloud of witnesses, let us lay aside every weight, and the sin which so easily ensnares us, and let us run with endurance the race that is set before us, looking unto Jesus, the author and finisher of our faith, who for the joy that was set before Him endured the cross, despising the shame, and has sat down at the right hand of the throne of God. For consider Him who endured such hostility from sinners against Himself, lest you become weary and discouraged in your souls" (Hebrews 12:1-3).

Looking upon the Lord Jesus is a wonderful antidote to pride and consequential discontentment. In the same way that humility leads to contentment then pride inevitably produces a lack of contentment. When we think highly of ourselves then we will always think that we should have more and are deserving of better. We look at adverts and believe that it should be us in that car, wearing those clothes, going to those hotels and enjoying that sin. However, when we look at Christ it is a wakeup call. There was no one on earth more deserving of praise, worship or possessions than Him. As the creator and sustainer of all things he had the right to a better everything. As the only perfect sinless man who ever lived he should not have been living in obscurity in Nazareth wearing the clothes of a carpenter and living in a humble house. For the biggest part of His life our Lord Jesus displayed perfect contentment with humble circumstances. He wasn't special in his own community. He didn't stand out as exceptional and He certainly didn't get the respect that was his right. He was a humble man and content with an ordinary life. His example is a powerful lesson in proper humility.

It is interesting that before psychologists thought about introspective analysis and self this that or the other we can see the wisdom of God displayed in this area. According to John, "Jesus, knowing that the Father had given all things into His hands, and that He had come from God and was going to God, rose from supper and laid aside His garments, took a towel and girded Himself. After that, He poured water into a basin and began to wash the disciples' feet, and to wipe them with the towel with which He was girded" (John 13:3-5). The Lord had perfect knowledge of who He was and what He was and unlike anyone else it was essentially good. He had come from God and was going back to God. Even with that knowledge He washed his disciples feet and displayed deep humility. If we gain an understanding of who and what we are we must humble ourselves.

Humility is the soil in which contentment grows and is only present when we are focused on the Lord Jesus and not on ourselves. We need to think of Him, love Him, serve Him, worship Him, please Him, read of Him and realise He is more important to us than we are to ourselves. We surely ought to find our joy, ambition, life goals, meaning and relevance in Christ. It is true freedom to yield to His will and worship Him so that all our significance is found in our relationship with Him and service for Him. Christians who are leading a quiet life for God have turned their backs on the ethos of our age which excludes God and His truth and have stopped bothering with introspective meditation, life goals, self-esteem or strategies to overcome perceived weakness which never get to the root problem of sin.

It is liberating to humble ourselves under the mighty hand of God and be content with a quiet life. To find in our quiet ordinariness the simple joy of living like the carpenter who humbled himself, working with his own hands until he was 30 and doing no miracle until the wedding at Cana of Galilee. This was the same man who stood at Jordan and heard God His Father express delight in his quiet ordinary life that had been lived under the gaze of Heaven and had brought pleasure to the heart of God.

CHAPTER SEVEN

Mind Your Own Business

It is a familiar expression usually aimed at a nosy person and delivered with a hint of righteous indignation. Depending on where you live there might be variations of the refrain but I suspect that most of us know what is meant. It does seem to have been a problem in Thessalonica with Paul returning to the subject in his second letter, "for we hear that there are some who walk among you in a disorderly manner, not working at all, but are busybodies" (2 Thessalonians 3:11). Busybody is a word that conjures up in my mind an old woman fussing about some irrelevant piece of gossip. It doesn't convey to me a big problem or a terribly destructive person. However, when you start reading what the Bible says about this type of behaviour you soon discover the terrible harm done by meddling in other people's business. It is an altogether different picture of gossip, hypocrisy, jealousy and trouble.

Paul linked the issue to laziness and a reluctance to work. In Thessalonica this had spiritual camouflage with people taking the view that they were waiting for the Lord to come back at any moment so why should they work. Since the Lord had not come back "the devil was finding work for idle hands to do". The result was that a positive of living in the anticipation of the Lord's return was being turned into a negative by some people taking it beyond apostolic instruction and going too far. Does it sound familiar? People had too little about which to concern themselves and were getting involved in an inappropriate way in other people's lives.

I am one of those people who don't like dogs and am also that person whom dogs don't like. It is not a great combination and I think they can sense my discomfort. You know the scenario, you go into someone's house and they love their dog. It is like a member of the family and is given free run of the house. It sniffs around under the dinner table and tries to slobber all over your trousers. As it jumps up on you and makes your clothes smell, covering you with hairs, the owner is smiling benignly and telling you that it is just being friendly and won't bite. I try and keep my hands away from dogs and have no desire to clap them or tickle their belly as they roll around in front of me. I don't like the friendliest of dogs.

Sometimes when I am out walking and passing a garden gate a dog, or wild beast depending on your perspective, jumps about barking madly. After I have recovered my poise I usually just keep walking, muttering something unpleasant under my breath. I have never and will never lean over the gate and take the dog by the ears, with good reason. There is a proverb which says that "he who passes by and meddles in a quarrel not his own is like one who takes a dog by the ears" (Proverbs 26:17). It is not a good idea and will end badly.

The wise writer of the Proverbs used the thought of taking a dog by the ears to describe the folly of meddling in a quarrel between other people. "Sticking your nose in where it doesn't belong and is not welcome" to put it in the polite version of the Scottish vernacular. It is not going to end well. It is not wise to get involved when other people are quarrelling, if you can avoid it. There are circumstances which demand involvement if you are drawn into the issue by various legitimate means and circumstances. However, unless we are brought in, or have a responsibility to get involved, it is better to mind our own business. How many quarrels have escalated in the local church or family context because those involved were not left to resolve the issue without interference? Often the initial cause of the quarrel is forgotten and the issue then becomes the conduct of those who got involved. People take sides and battle lines are drawn. An issue, which could have been resolved between two people becomes something much bigger and more complex. Life would be so much quieter, calmer, less stressful with much less drama if we just didn't get involved in what doesn't concern us.

There is an assumption in the expression that is easily overlooked. While we should not meddle in other people's business we ought to make sure we take care of our own. It could be that we are not the people we should be because we spend too much time concerned about what other people are doing rather than concentrating on our own walk with the Lord. Peter fell into this trap as he spoke to the Lord Jesus. Looking at John, his fellow disciple, he said to Jesus, "But Lord, what about this man?" Jesus said to him, "If I will that he remain till I come, what is that to you? You follow Me." (John 21:21, 22). Peter was being told in no uncertain terms to mind his own business and that meant keeping his nose out of John's business but also concentrating on his own walk as a disciple. Peter would have enough on his plate serving and following without any distractions. Saul of Tarsus expressed the right idea on the Damascus road, "So he, trembling and astonished, said, "Lord, what do You want me to do?" (Acts 9:6).

With all of these exhortations there is a balance that prevents extremes. In the same way that a quiet life should not be an excuse for isolation, minding your own business does not mean indifference to other people's needs. There is a significant difference between loving other people and meddling in their business. An important part of Christianity is the sharing and caring that comes with true fellowship. Throughout the New Testament there are many scriptures that teach the necessity of putting the interests and needs of others as a greater priority than our own. Philippians Chapters 2, cites the example of the Lord Jesus, exhorting each of us to "look out not only for his own interests, but also for the interests of others" (Philippians 2:4). When Paul wrote to the Galatian churches he taught the Christians to "bear one another's burdens, and so fulfil the law of Christ" (Galatians 6:2). I could fill these pages citing scriptures that teach us to actively love one another and not merely to express sentiments in fluffy words.

I recently made one of these wonderful little discoveries when I was listening to a sermon by John MacArthur on 1 Corinthians Chapter 13. He pointed out that the root Greek word from which "kind" is derived means to "be helpful". I enjoyed that thought. Love is expressed in deeds of kindness which are useful. Thinking about that aspect of love brought me to the conclusion that loving people in our immediate circumstances requires us to be involved with each other. If you have a superficial relationship with other people you will never get to know their problems and concerns. It will be hard to love them in a useful manner since your knowledge of their circumstances will be limited. You may have experienced the well-meaning efforts of someone trying to help you but they don't really know you and can sometimes just make the matter worse. Biblical love is best expressed when we get up close and personal with each other. That does not preclude us loving others who live in different places and helping them in their need by prayer or practical expressions of fellowship. But for the people in our community, church, family or workplace the great example for us is the Lord Jesus who could not have come any closer or got more involved than he did when he left Heaven and came right down to where we were. Long distance love it most certainly was not, "And the Word became flesh and dwelt among us" (John 1:14). He lived among those he came to love and serve. Of all the places he could have lived, he chose Nazareth, and of all the places in society he could have occupied, he worked as a carpenter.

Here is the conundrum, on the one hand we have to mind our own business but on the other hand we have to love each other. How can you do the one and the other? Keeping your nose out of someone's business and yet loving that person which demands involvement beyond a superficial relationship. How do we catch the right balance?

Motive is the key. Why do I want to know? What will I do with what I know? Am I meddling, curious, nosy or do I have a genuine love and care that wants to share the burden and encourage. With sensitivity I can make sure that you know I am interested in you for all the right reasons and build a relationship of trust. I can help you, pray for you and with you, support, encourage, love and most importantly, talk to you and not about you.

Alternatively, I can seek information for all the wrong reasons. Put simply I can be interested in you so that I can gossip about you. It is one of the most insidious sins and wears all sorts of dressing up outfits. It appears as a Good Samaritan, a praying saint, a concerned friend, a responsible elder, a wise sage or any number of disguises. Underneath them all can lurk this destructive poison. It is worth reading some of the wise Proverbs that speak about the talebearer.

"A talebearer reveals secrets, But he who is of a faithful spirit conceals a matter" (Proverbs 11:13).

"The words of a talebearer are like tasty trifles, And they go down into the inmost body (Proverbs 18:8).

"He who goes about as a talebearer reveals secrets; Therefore do not associate with one who flatters with his lips" (Proverbs 20:19).

In my experience one of the outcomes of gossip is that the person being maligned is denied a quiet life. Gossip can bring a storm of trouble crashing around someone's head filling his circumstances with clamour and noise.

All of my adult life I have wanted to have a real fire in my living room. This was the year it happened. A wood burning stove now has pride of place in my living room and I love to play with it. There is nothing quite like the crackle and smell of wood burning on a cold winter's evening. I quickly realised that this pleasure required a bit of work since I was going through wood at a shocking rate. My friend Wallace Hewitson obliged and built me a nice log store in my back garden. The challenge is to keep it full. Without a steady flow of wood into that store my fire will be cold. It is the same with gossip. "Where there is no wood, the fire goes out; And where there is no talebearer, strife ceases" (Proverbs 26:20). Strife is the enemy of a quiet life. If you have ever been caught up in strife you will know how all consuming it can be. You think about the trouble all the time and it eats away at your peace of mind. Strife consumes a person so that their worship dries up and their relationships suffer. A sense of injustice and frustration can roar in your mind as strife licks around your feet like a fire with that "friend" or "concerned person" throwing on the wood of self-righteous gossip.

Minding our own business would stop so much strife among Christians. Problems would be contained among those immediately concerned. Issues in a local church or family would remain within that church or family. Misunderstandings, exaggerations, lies, misinformation, pride and hypocrisy would not flourish as they can when we get involved in something which has nothing to do with us.

In our modern social media age the opportunity for meddling is at an all time high. I can blog, comment or make uninformed observations from afar like the crowd at the gladiatorial games. I may even go beyond shouting abuse and decide that I am Caesar. I will raise or lower my proverbial thumb as if what I think is of any consequence or relevance. In the meantime the sense of my own importance grows at an alarming rate as I count the likes on Facebook or comments on my blog. My sinful pride balloons as I throw gossipy wood on the fire of someone else's misery. Shame on us if we condemn the Pharisees for bringing the woman taken in adultery before the Lord Jesus for condemnation while our fingers skip over the keyboard with gleeful delight pouring out our ignorant poison. If you have ever been on the receiving end of such abuse you would never get involved.

There is a causal connection between minding your own business, gossip and hypocrisy. The nose is connected to the tongue which alters the face. When your nose is in the wrong place your tongue starts to work in all the wrong ways and you end up with two faces. The essence of hypocrisy is to be two faced. We listen with concern, make sympathetic inquiry, ask all sorts of penetrating questions and then slip that mask off and put on the other one that was behind our back. The text is sent, the group chat started, the feigned sorrow and pity as we spread the confidences and add a little bit of spice here and there.

The Lord Jesus told a parable which is recorded in Luke chapter 6 in which one of the metaphors used is almost comic strip stuff. "And why do you look at the speck in your brother's eye, but do not perceive the plank in your own eye? Or how can you say to your brother, 'Brother, let me remove the speck that is in your eye,' when you yourself do not see the plank that is in your own eye?

Hypocrite! First remove the plank from your own eye, and then you will see clearly to remove the speck that is in your brother's eye" (Luke 6:41, 42).

Just picture the scene. I am standing with a long plank of wood sticking out of my eye and I am looking at you. Anyone looking at us would say that I have a serious problem that needs immediate attention. I am the only person who thinks otherwise. I have no awareness that I have a plank sticking out of my eye but I do have concerns about you. I am aware that you have a speck of dust in your eye and it is troubling me. It isn't troubling you but in my thinking something needs to be done about that speck and I am just the person to get involved. Now clearly I should be more concerned about my problem which is so obviously more serious. In addition, my problem is going to impair my ability to help you in your much smaller issue. If I have a plank in my eye my vision will be impaired and my ability to remove a speck from your eye will be adversely affected.

The parable is a deliberately exaggerated scenario to make a point. So often we are just as ridiculous in the way we try to get involved in other people's problems when we have serious issues of our own. Our hypocrisy can know no end. With righteous indignation we observe some failing in another person and think we should text, blog, gossip and generally spread the word far and near. How different was the response of David to the news that his enemy King Saul and his good friend Jonathan had fallen in battle. "Tell it not in Gath, Proclaim it not in the streets of Ashkelon-- Lest the daughters of the Philistines rejoice, Lest the daughters of the uncircumcised triumph"

(2 Samuel 1:20). Don't heap misery on another person's grief.

So often our own hypocrisy is of a far greater magnitude then the sin that we see in others. The plank is well and truly jutting out of our eye as we begin our conversation "have you heard about ...." Then it begins and someone's quiet life is disturbed as the word spreads. What we should always remember is that what goes around comes around. That is the way it works and soon my quiet life could be shattered. "But let none of you suffer as a murderer, a thief, an evildoer, or as a busybody in other people's matters" (1 Peter 4:15). Better to mind my own business.

CHAPTER EIGHT

Work With Your Own Hands

Work is Good

As a Scot who was born on the West side of Scotland I am well aware of the "the Protestant work ethic". I recently came across a paper, "Religion, the Scottish work ethic and the spirit of enterprise" written by Robert Smith. It is an academic critique of Max Weber's work "The Protestant Ethic and the Spirit of Capitalism" dealing with the historical connection between Calvinistic Presbyterianism and the value placed upon hard graft in Scotland. A quote from the abstract at the beginning of the paper gives a taste of some of Smith's conclusions. "The Scottish work ethic is a secularized drive peculiar to Scotland with its strong Calvinistic religious heritage and emphasis on hard work, thrift and education". Not bad! I don't mean that every morning all around Scotland there are crowds of people standing in trains and trudging along pavements like the seven dwarfs singing "Hi ho, hi ho.". ! I think it is also fair to say that you would have to be wearing large nationalistic blinkers to think that the work ethic is a uniquely Scottish attribute.

At the beginning of the Bible God introduces Himself as a worker. Genesis begins with God forming the heavens and earth over six days and resting on the seventh. He is very different from the gods of the ancient pagan myths who were capricious, lazy and selfish beings. The God of the Bible introduces himself as a worker who creates incredible beauty, complexity and order from nothing. There is no other week's work that can compare to the creative work of God. Laws of nature were put into place; matter, atomic structure, energy, light, atmosphere, oceans, ecology, life, the list is endless and then, of course, in a few words God tells us that "he made the stars also". It has to be the greatest understatement on paper: a seemingly throwaway statement explains the origin of humanity's ultimate fascination, which we call "space".

God does not stop working from Genesis to Revelation. He created a wife for Adam and maintained His creation. It is in God that we live and move and have our being, according to the preaching of Paul. It is God who upholds all things by the word of his power (Heb 1:3). Following His creative work we are introduced to his redemptive work, which continues to this day. God is always working and that is why the Lord Jesus said that "My Father has been working until now, and I have been working" (John 5:17).

When God made Adam he did so in His own image and likeness (Genesis 1:26). I am not sure I fully understand what that means but I do know that if God is a worker then He created us to be workers. This is evident from God's instructions to Adam in the early days of Eden before sin entered the world. Work was never a consequence of sin or a punishment meted out to mankind as a result of their disobedience. It was not God's intention to create man in order for him to be lying about in paradise eating fruit from lots of trees and chilling out for ever. God charged Adam with the care of Eden, "Then the LORD God took the man and put him in the garden of Eden to tend and keep it "(Genesis 2:15). Before sin entered the world and things went very bad, everything was good and God was satisfied with what he had done. Adam had dominion over the creation and was tasked with working in the garden. As God saw Adam in that environment he declared that it was not good for man to be alone and gave Adam help to do his work by making the first woman. "And the LORD God said, "It is not good that man should be alone; I will make him a helper comparable to him" (Genesis 2:18).

I came across an interesting article in the "Theology of Work Project, Inc." and specifically by Andrew Schmutzer and Alice Mathews who are contributors to that project. The article is entitled, "People are created in God's Image" and explores the connection between God's creative work and man's work within that creation. I would encourage you to explore the Theology of Work web site which provides a valuable resource hub on the subject and explores it in more detail than is my intention in this book.

Work remains a good thing and God expects us to work. When we become Christians that does not change, despite what some of the Thessalonians seemed to think.

Hard Work

If work is a good thing why is it so hard? It is perhaps in the sphere of work more than any other area of our lives that problems, pressure, exhaustion and anxiety arise. We may accept that work is necessary but most people look forward to the day when they retire. We admire people that don't need to work. So what has changed? Why is it so hard?

If we turn our thoughts back to Genesis ch3 we get the answer. We have spent some time in an earlier chapter dealing with Satan disturbing Adam and Eve's ordinary lives. When he had done his work Adam and Eve were left to face the consequences of their actions. God spoke firstly to Eve about the impact of sin in the principal sphere of her responsibility. The conception of children would be multiplied and childbearing would be painful. Her relationship with Adam was also going to feel the impact of the battle of the sexes as she would find his authority irksome and try to resist it. "To the woman He said: "I will greatly multiply your sorrow and your conception; In pain you shall bring forth children; Your desire shall be for your husband, And he shall rule over you" (Genesis 3:16).

The Lord then spoke to Adam and explained that his principal sphere of responsibility as a man and a husband would be impacted by sin. Work was going to get hard. "Then to Adam He said, "Because you have heeded the voice of your wife, and have eaten from the tree of which I commanded you, saying, 'You shall not eat of it': "Cursed is the ground for your sake; In toil you shall eat of it All the days of your life. Both thorns and thistles it shall bring forth for you, And you shall eat the herb of the field. In the sweat of your face you shall eat bread till you return to the ground, For out of it you were taken; For dust you are, And to dust you shall return" (Genesis 3:17-19). God did not curse work and make it a bad thing but he did curse the ground and make it a hard thing. Sin was the reason why work got hard and that curse remains on the ground today.

Work is not easy, but Paul reminded Timothy of our responsibility to work and provide for our families, "But if anyone does not provide for his own, and especially for those of his household, he has denied the faith and is worse than an unbeliever" (1 Timothy 5:8). That is strong stuff from Paul. Providing for those under our care is something that people who are not Christians recognise as the right thing to do. As Christians we have no excuse; we don't rely on our own sense of right and wrong but have the objective standard of God written down for us in the Bible.

Paul wanted to prevent some of the Thessalonians developing a dependence culture in the church. It was good in the early days of the Church when the believers had all things common and helped to support each other. It is also good when the strong support the weak and express mutual care. However we should not expect to be supported by the hard work of others with a sense of entitlement. When Paul wrote his second letter to the Thessalonian church he reminded them of what they had heard him teach, "For even when we were with you, we commanded you this: If anyone will not work, neither shall he eat" (2 Thessalonians 3:10). He was conscious of his example to the new Christians and on occasions supported himself by working with his hands. He had been in Ephesus for some time and when he met with the Ephesians elders as he travelled to Rome he reminded them "I have coveted no one's silver or gold or apparel. Yes, you yourselves know that these hands have provided for my necessities, and for those who were with me. I have shown you in every way, by labouring like this, that you must support the weak. And remember the words of the Lord Jesus, that He said, 'It is more blessed to give than to receive'" (Acts 20:33-35).

When the Bible speaks of work it does not refer to a specific job or career. It does speak about the effort and application that ought to characterise us in our work, whatever it may be. It is important to remember that work does not always mean employment. You don't have to have a job to work. Many forms of work, which are not paid employment, meet the needs of family or community. God puts no pressure on Christians to earn big money, but we are to work to support ourselves, our families, our local church and do what we can for the community.

If you want to do a study on what God has to say about hard work then look at the Sluggard in the Bible. There are many other scriptures dealing with the subject and I have referenced a small selection below.

He who tills his land will be satisfied with bread, But he who follows frivolity is devoid of understanding.
(Proverbs 12:11)

In all labour there is profit, But idle chatter leads only to poverty.
(Proverbs 14:23)

He who is slothful in his work Is a brother to him who is a great destroyer.
(Proverbs 18:9)

The lazy man will not plow because of winter; He will beg during harvest and have nothing.
(Proverbs 20:4)

So I perceived that nothing is better than that a man should rejoice in his own works, for that is his heritage. For who can bring him to see what will happen after him?
(Ecclesiastes 3:22)

Whatever your hand finds to do, do it with your might; for there is no work or device or knowledge or wisdom in the grave where you are going.
(Ecclesiastes 9:10)

Bondservants, obey in all things your masters according to the flesh, not with eyeservice, as men-pleasers, but in sincerity of heart, fearing God. And whatever you do, do it heartily, as to the Lord and not to men.
(Colossians 3:22, 23)

Both the Apostle Paul, who was not afraid of rolling his sleeves up and working as a tent maker when the occasion demanded, and the Lord Jesus, who spent most of his life working as a carpenter in Nazareth, have left examples as well as instruction about how to work.

Secular or Spiritual

It would be a mistake to think in terms of secular and

spiritual work. Perhaps when you think of your week you think of the spiritual weekend and the secular week. The Bible does not make that distinction. All work is seen as spiritual whether you are preaching, studying the Bible, praying, caring for people, working in a factory, sitting at a desk, serving in a shop or running a business. There is no such thing as secular work for the Christian.

Being a Christian does not make work any easier. The effect of the curse pronounced on the earth in Genesis ch3 is still effective. It requires effort on our part to put food on the table and a roof over the heads of our family. For the vast majority of Christians work means long shifts, worry, effort and basic hard graft. The difference lies in the added spiritual dimension. This means that as a Christian I need to appreciate that God is interested in my working life. What I achieve Monday to Thursday and how I conduct myself is a significant factor in my spiritual welfare.

I mentioned the words of the Lord to Adam which seem to suggest a futility to a working life. He said "In the sweat of your face you shall eat bread Till you return to the ground, For out of it you were taken; For dust you are, And to dust you shall return" (Genesis 3:19). Without God in your life there is no real point to work beyond the immediate goal of obtaining resources to provide for your dependants. You earn enough money to get some nice stuff or have some nice experiences but then it is back to work. Adam was told that he was formed from the ground, would spend his life digging the ground and then be put back into the ground. When you take away the sophistication that we have draped like camouflage over the reality of our existence, without God and the Gospel there is nothing more than futility. This was the conclusion of the Preacher at the beginning of Ecclesiastes.

"Vanity of vanities," says the Preacher; "Vanity of vanities, all is vanity."
What profit has a man from all his labour In which he toils under the sun?
One generation passes away, and another generation comes; But the earth abides forever.
The sun also rises, and the sun goes down, And hastens to the place where it arose.
The wind goes toward the south, And turns around to the north; The wind whirls about continually, And comes again on its circuit.
All the rivers run into the sea, Yet the sea is not full; To the place from which the rivers come, There they return again.
All things are full of labour; Man cannot express it. The eye is not satisfied with seeing, Nor the ear filled with hearing.
That which has been is what will be, That which is done is what will be done, And there is nothing new under the sun.
Is there anything of which it may be said, "See, this is new"? It has already been in ancient times before us.
There is no remembrance of former things, Nor will there be any remembrance of things that are to come By those who will come after.
(Ecclesiastes 1:2-11)

We may be digging in the dirt of IT, manufacturing, services, communication, entertainment or whatever area of the economy in which we work but essentially we are digging and the sweat is pouring off our brow until the day arrives when we put down our shovel and wait to be put into the ground. It sounds fatalistic, but without God what else is there? Some people convince themselves that they are doing something for a new generation or advancing the cause of this, that or the other and that may be right. However, no matter what benefits are achieved for others through our work, the day will come when we will walk away from the office for the last time and will quickly fade from memory.

Work may not be easier for Christians but our work has spiritual significance. It is much more than giving us the contacts that enable us to do some of the "spiritual things" that we normally do at the weekend. Our work is a spiritual activity and as a result our perspective ought to be different from someone who does not serve God. Work is different for a Christian, if not easier.

When I was young I would spend hours reading books on the wars of the 19th and 20th centuries. As I got older I found the history of the Church interesting, especially as it helps us to understand how we have arrived at our fractured and weak condition in the 21st century. Throughout church history as in all history, significant changes from the established norms of the day were usually associated with one or two people that God used to change the status quo. Martin Luther was such a man. He was a German monk who played a significant role in the Protestant Reformation of the 16th century. Being a monk and a highly influential one at that, you might have expected him to extol the virtue of prayer and Bible study as God's work and everything else as a secondary occupation. Nothing could be further from the truth. He taught the spiritual virtue of work. "Your work is a very sacred matter. God delights in it, and through it he wants to bestow his blessings on you. This praise of work should be inscribed on all tools, on the forehead and faces that sweat from toiling"

The story goes that a cobbler asked Luther how he could glorify God as a Christian. Luther's answer was not that the cobbler should sell a "Christian shoe," but rather that he should make a good shoe and sell it at a fair price. Martin Luther taught that people should use the gifts that God gave them in loving service to their neighbour. Christian cobblers, Luther said in effect, should not make shoes with little crosses on them - they should make the best shoes they can and sell them at a fair price so their neighbours can have good shoes.

Work is worship

Worship can be a narrow concept among Christians today. If you asked some believers what a worship leader did in their Church I am certain they would refer to music or singing. I think it would be rare to describe a Bible teacher as a worship leader and even rarer for the person who organizes for the bins to be collected every week or washes the windows and cleans the church building to be described this way. We don't associate worship with menial day to day tasks unless they are bookended by hymns and prayer. There are good books on worship that touch this point and explain in clear terms that worship comes from every aspect of our lives. It is more than what we say or sing. Paul speaks about offering our body as a living sacrifice and takes worship to another level. It is the sacrifice of ourselves, everything we are and have, given to God as His rightful due. John MacArthur's book with the self-explanatory title "Worship: The Ultimate Priority" is well worth reading in this connection.

Many of us readily accept that weekend work when the local church is gathered together is worship. We can see that whoever is doing whatever around the church services, building or in the name of the church in the community is worshipping God. We see the closed eyes and furrowed brow of earnest prayer, we listen to the passionate voices straining to capture the pathos of a hymn. We value the reliable and committed members of the Church who are always there. It looks and feels like worship.

When it comes to Monday morning and you are standing at the shop counter, in the warehouse, on the boat, at the workshop, team meeting, sales conference or whatever your work environment may be, it doesn't feel like worship. You may be sitting in the middle of the most ungodly atmosphere listening to things that you would rather not hear and being asked to do things that are giving you conscience issues. The conversation may all be about money, company politics, targets, figures and pressure. You may be the only person in the room or organization who believes there is a God never mind having a desire to worship Him. Work done in that environment doesn't feel like worship.

Work is worship when it is done as unto the Lord. Paul developed this thought in Ephesians ch5. He was dealing with the need for Christians to be submissive in their relationships and began with husbands and wives, moved on to children and parents and ended up with masters and servants. Amongst other things he emphasized that when a servant was obedient to his master he was rendering service to the Lord. "Not with eyeservice, as men-pleasers, but as bondservants of Christ, doing the will of God from the heart, with goodwill doing service, as to the Lord, and not to men" (Ephesians 6:6, 7). Paul was teaching the Ephesians that when we serve an earthly master we are actually serving our heavenly Master. The Lord accepts our work as worship since we are his bondservants and work as if we were reporting directly to Him rather than our immediate employer. The incentive for us is that our work receives immediate recompense in the form of wages but because it is rendered to our Lord it will also receive recompense from Him in a coming day. "Knowing that whatever good anyone does, he will receive the same from the Lord, whether he is a slave or free" (Ephesians 6:8).

What does it look like when we apply Ephesians ch5 to our work, bearing in mind that our work may be done in the context of employment, self employment, our home, community, paid or unpaid. If we think about the home sphere and the work involved in caring for family and being a homemaker, it can be repetitive and unappreciated. I think back to my upbringing when our mother worked hard in the house throughout our school years. It is fair to say that I didn't appreciate her work and didn't give any thought to the process of washing and ironing and putting clothes away. As boys we launched our clothes into a corner of our room and hey presto when we woke up they were gone and somehow reappeared in our drawers washed and neatly folded. That was the result of my mother working hard without any appreciation from us who benefited from her work. I didn't think too much about the process of cooking and cleaning but reaped the benefits of my mother's hard work every evening when we sat down to eat dinner as a family in a clean house. Although my mother didn't get a lot of thanks from her boys for her daily work she was worshipping God. Worship is essentially an obedient response to God. Scripture teaches a mother "to love their husbands, to love their children, to be discreet, chaste, homemakers, good, obedient to their own husbands, that the word of God may not be blasphemed" (Titus 2:4, 5). Diligent obedience to those commands is worship. When we realize that God notices our work at home and among our family it should change our attitude to what seems repetitive and unappreciated. When we do even the smallest tasks as unto the Lord, He receives them as worship of equal value to eloquent prayers or spine tingling singing. "And whatever you do, do it heartily, as to the Lord and not to men" (Colossians 3:23).

In the context of suffering, Peter wrote to servants about their work. He was addressing household servants who often suffered with no employment rights, grievance procedures or unions to fight their case. In the most difficult circumstances he encouraged servants to see the spiritual dimension to their work. "Servants, be submissive to your masters with all fear, not only to the good and gentle, but also to the harsh" (1 Peter 2:18). Why should a servant submit to a master who was unreasonable or abusive? Peter explained that such submission was an act of worship, "For this is commendable, if because of conscience toward God one endures grief, suffering wrongfully. For what credit is it if, when you are beaten for your faults, you take it patiently? But when you do good and suffer, if you take it patiently, this is commendable before God" (1 Peter 2:19, 20).

I remember when I was working as a solicitor in Glasgow and was assigned to work as an assistant to a partner in the legal firm. He was a challenge due to his fiery temper and irrational behaviour. I remember times when he was under pressure and threw the telephone and various other objects about his office. He was not the easiest of individuals and submitting to him was sometimes the last thing that I wanted to do. I may have been able to work better in these circumstances if I had appreciated a little more of the spiritual dimension to my work.

The Christians to whom Peter wrote were enduring far worse problems in their work than I ever did. As they got on with their work and continued to serve in these difficult circumstances they were worshipping God by their submission to their earthly masters. In a modern context our employment is very different from that of Roman slaves. We have rights and procedures which by and large protect us from employers' abuse. However, the principle remains that as we work for reasonable or unreasonable employers God is well pleased when we work hard and submit to our employers' authority. It is amazing to think that we can bring pleasure to the heart of God by the way we approach our work. God will be pleased when he sees us quietly and diligently working, which means that we can please God at work as well as on Sunday morning.

Work is Witness

Our work can give us opportunities to witness by bringing us into close relationship with people whom we would otherwise never meet. We can show kindness, compassion, honesty and by so doing open their ears to the Gospel.

"The Lord Jesus did not, as incarnate, live a life of detachment. He lived a life of involvement. He lived where he could see human sin, hear human swearing and blasphemy, see human diseases and observe human mortality, poverty and squalor. His mission was fully incarnational because he taught men by coming alongside them, becoming one of them and sharing their environment and their problems".
(Donald McLeod, A Faith To Live By).

For most of us, it is at work more than any other place in our lives that we are in close proximity to people who are not Christians. There is a tremendous opportunity in your school, factory, office or shop to be a good witness for the Lord Jesus by displaying a Christlike attitude to work, other workers and your employer. When Paul wrote to Titus he emphasised this important aspect to witness in the work environment. "Exhort bondservants to be obedient to their own masters, to be well pleasing in all things, not answering back, not pilfering, but showing all good fidelity, that they may adorn the doctrine of God our Saviour in all things" (Titus 2:9, 10). Paul was exhorting servants to display the doctrine of God in their work.

There is no point speaking about the transforming power of your God if there is no transformation in your life. On the other hand if there is evidence of a difference between you and your fellow employees it will provoke interest and perhaps give you the opportunity to speak about the Gospel. We should be aware that how we live in our work place directly affects our witness. We are "an epistle ... known and read by all men" (2 Corinthians 3:2, 3). It would be great if people knew we were Christians before we told them and we were good ambassadors of Jesus Christ. When Luke began the Acts of the Apostles he referred to "all that Jesus began both to do and teach" (Acts 1:1). There was perfect harmony between what he said and did. Without such consistency between conduct and conversation we undermine the Gospel.

As we work we are worshipping God and witnessing to the world. We bring pleasure to God by working "as unto the Lord". In close proximity to other people we display the doctrine of the Gospel in our character and righteous conduct, treating our colleagues with respect and submitting to our employer with humility and integrity. When we turn up for work, rather than simply digging in the dirt, we are fulfilling the Lord's commission in the unreached world of our staff room, work bench, classroom, van, office or factor. "And He said to them, "Go into all the world and preach the gospel to every creature" (Mark 16:15).

CHAPTER NINE

The Effect Of An Ordinary Life

If you are like me, you will be interested to observe the carrot that Paul places before the Thessalonians having exhorted them to work hard, mind their own business and live quietly in their community. What does that type of life produce? What is the incentive that will encourage a positive response from them and from us? In concluding this short, sharp reminder of his previous command to them, Paul encourages them by explaining the impact of their ordinary lives on "those who are outside" as well as on their own quality of life.

"That you may walk properly toward those who are outside, and that you may lack nothing" (1 Thessalonians 4:12).

"Those who are outside" is an interesting way to describe a group of people and does have a ring of The Hunger Games about it. It is a simple concept used mainly by Paul when he is drawing a distinction between believers and non-believers.

In 1 Corinthians ch5 Paul is giving instruction to the Corinthian church about dealing with a Christian who is in the church and is committing sexual sin. The course of action that the church must take involves distancing themselves from the person in question, to the extent that they must break off all contact with him in order to lead him to repentance and restoration. Paul makes clear that this does not mean that they should have no dealings with non-Christian people who commit the same sin as the disciplined church member. They must make a distinction between those who are outside the church and those who are inside. "For what have I to do with judging those also who are outside? Do you not judge those who are inside" (1 Corinthians 5:12)?

He makes the same distinction, though he does not explicitly use the word "outside" or "outsider", when he speaks about the impact the evident presence of God would have on onlookers when there was the orderly use of spiritual gifts in their church gatherings "Therefore if the whole church comes together in one place, and all speak with tongues, and there come in those who are uninformed or unbelievers, will they not say that you are out of your mind? But if all prophesy, and an unbeliever or an uninformed person comes in, he is convinced by all, he is convicted by all. And thus the secrets of his heart are revealed; and so, falling down on his face, he will worship God and report that God is truly among you" (1 Corinthians 14:23-25).

David Mathis has an excellent blog post on the Desiring God website dealing with various scriptures which explain why we should care what outsiders think. It is worth quoting, "Care for outsiders goes beyond First Corinthians. Related is the healthy concern for the gospel's reputation in the Pastoral Epistles. Whether it's the conduct of widows (1 Timothy 5:14), slaves (1

Timothy 6:1; Titus 2:10), or young women (Titus 2:5), Paul would have us seek 'in everything [to] adorn the doctrine of God our Saviour' (Titus 2:10) and not bring any just reviling on the name, teaching, and word of God (1 Timothy 6:1; Titus 2:5). He would have us be concerned to 'show perfect courtesy toward all people' (Titus 3:2), and have us care that our good works 'are excellent and profitable for people' (Titus 3:8)".

Our reputation among our neighbours, colleagues and family is very important. It matters how we treat each other and care for widows; the spiritual temperature of our church gatherings does make a difference when we invite other people among us; our righteous conduct in business will either defame or enhance the Gospel we preach in the thinking of those who listen; our good works will deprive our spiritual enemies of ammunition in the ongoing conflict (1 Peter 1:21).

I am going to quote Mathis again as he focuses our attention on the question, should we care what outsiders think? "The biblical answer is just as much yes (if not more so) as it is no. But most significant is why, and both the apostle's example and his exhortation agree: that they may be saved. 'Give no offense, either to the Jews or to the Greeks or to the church of God, just as I also please all men in all things, not seeking my own profit, but the profit of many, that they may be saved' (1 Corinthians 10:32, 33). In the end, we care because God cares. He delights to make outsiders into insiders. He rejoices to bend his heart outward to the vilest offender, and not to leave them outside, but bring them into the sphere of his eternal covenant love".

Paul is telling the Thessalonians that a proper walk before the ungodly is a sincere ordinary life. It is that which will make an impression on people and even although the Gospel may be offensive to them they will be impressed by the integrity of our lives to the extent that they will glorify God. "Having your conduct honorable among the Gentiles, that when they speak against you as evildoers, they may, by your good works which they observe, glorify God in the day of visitation" (1 Peter 2:12).

In Thessalonica some of the Christians were in danger of bringing the Gospel into disrepute by their conduct. When they gave up their work in anticipation of the Lord's return they were giving unnecessary ammunition to the enemies of the Cross. They would look foolish if the Lord did not come and they were conveying the wrong impression of Christianity by not working and just waiting.

We often overlook the powerful impact of an ordinary life. It is a stronger testimony than persuasive words without actions. It speaks of integrity, honesty and humility. We can be dazzled by the thought of the spectacular and by so doing forget that the vast majority of us are called to a humble ordinary life of work, family and church responsibility. Deep impressions are made upon unbelievers by our ordinary lives.

If the only benefit of living quietly, industriously and discreetly was a good testimony among "outsiders" then that would be reason enough to respond to Paul's exhortation. However, he goes further and explains that such a life is also greatly beneficial to us. We shall "lack nothing".

The outcome of hard work is generally a fair wage which meets our needs. If we work hard, keep humble and mind our own business we will likely keep in employment and remain self sufficient in terms of our material needs. There are always exceptions to this general principle. People lose their jobs through no fault of their own and because of circumstances far removed from their daily labour. There are some who cannot work due to disability or a lack of available work. The general rule is that people who do not keep a job for very long are either lazy, proud or lack contentment. They may agitate about their wage or opportunities. They may meddle in matters which are not their concern or they do not work hard enough to stay in the job.

An ordinary Christian life will mean that we are not reliant on others for the things which we ought to provide for ourselves. We will be dependent on God for the jobs to earn our "daily bread" and not be an unnecessary burden upon others.

CHAPTER TEN

A Tribute To An Ordinary Life

The Thessalonians believed that the Lord was coming back and they wanted to be ready. Rather than give up their work and spend time creating a stir in Thessalonica and chaos among the believers, Paul taught them to go to work, live a quiet life and keep their noses out of other people's business. For most of us that is what God calls us to do in our communities. There are some Christians are called by God to be missionaries in foreign countries, write best sellers, trend on twitter or preach to thousands, but not many.

I want to close this book with my experience of an ordinary life which was an exceptional testimony to people in a small community. I have met many people in different countries, have had the privilege of preaching with gifted orators and spending time with missionaries and writers. I have seen the influence of men and women in churches for good and bad and known some very charismatic people. I have never known a person who lived a very ordinary life and made such an impact for God as Jenny Leslie. I wouldn't expect many people who read this book to know Jenny. She was from Orkney and with her husband lived most of her life in Brae, Shetland.

I am typing this last page on the ferry to Shetland and I am sad. It was a week ago that I got the news that Jenny had passed to be with her Lord and her funeral is tomorrow. Jenny had been undergoing treatment for cancer for just over a year . During that time she was as remarkable as I expected her to be. Even in her illness she continued her ordinary walk with the Lord and witness to others. I remember sitting beside her bed with her husband Jimmy as she received her first round of chemotherapy in Aberdeen. It was a sobering and humbling experience as I watched Jenny speak to the nurses in her quiet and dignified way about the arrangements for her to fly back home. No fuss, just godly contentment to be in hands of her Lord for the dark days that lay ahead.

There was a period of my life when I visited Shetland 2 or 3 times a year to preach in the Gospel Halls. When I went to Brae for the first time I stayed with Jimmy and Jenny and that became my home from home in Shetland. I soon realised that Jenny was a remarkable woman. Jimmy and Jenny lived in a part of Brae where the houses are not big and quite close together. She worked in a small hardware store in the village and was a part of the community. She worked hard in that store and in her home kitchen. The smells that came up the stairs as I studied during the day always promised great things for dinnertime.

I soon came to accept that when I came down for breakfast in the morning there was every possibility that a neighbour would be sitting in the kitchen chatting to Jenny. On one visit it was always Christine, a desperate alcoholic who Jenny sat with, fed and helped above and beyond anything that could be called reasonable. There were others who came and chatted for ages and Jenny had patience that I had never seen before. I spoke to her about it and she didn't think it was remarkable at all. Then there were the trips to Lerwick and other places to help people who called her their friend.

Jenny read her Bible and prayed. She had Christianity Explored groups in her house for her neighbours. She loved and cared for her family. She worked hard and was not a gossip. People came and confided in her because they knew she loved them and would never harm them. She was content in Brae with her occasional forays down to see the family in Grangemouth and holidays in Wales. Her one complaint was always that she wanted a new kitchen. I remember getting the text when Jimmy eventually buckled and she got her new kitchen. It was her workplace and pulpit. I admired this godly woman who lived for others and I value the memory of times spent in her kitchen speaking about the Lord and listening to her wisdom as she spoke of her regrets about the past and hopes for the future.

Jenny Leslie lived an ordinary live, it was never mundane and was as selfless as I have ever witnessed. God never called her to write a book, be a missionary or cause a stir in Shetland. I know that in her ordinary life she accomplished much and has heard the commendation of her Lord, "Well done, good and faithful servant; you were faithful over a few things, I will make you ruler over many things. Enter into the joy of your lord" (Matthew 25:21).

Jenny taught me that great things are small things done regularly in love and sincerity and for that alone I will never forget my friend.

Of No Reputation

Of No Reputation

Of No Reputation

Of No Reputation

Of No Reputation